GENOCIDE

THE BASICS

WITHDRAWN FROM
THE LIBRARY
UNIVERSITY OF
WINCHESTER

Genocide: The Basics is an engaging introduction to the study of a controversial and widely debated topic. This concise and comprehensive book explores key questions such as "How successful have efforts been in the prevention of genocide?," "How prevalent has genocide been throughout history?" and "How has the concept been defined?"

Real world case studies address significant issues including:

- The killing of indigenous peoples by colonial powers;
- The Holocaust and the question of "uniqueness";
- Peacekeeping efforts in the 1990s;
- Legal attempts to create a genocide-free world.

With suggestions for further reading, discussion questions at the end of each chapter and a glossary of key terms, *Genocide: The Basics* is the ideal starting point for students approaching the topic for the first time.

Paul R. Bartrop is Professor of History and Director of the Center for Judaic, Holocaust, ar lf Coast University, Fort Myers, F

D1345033

KA 0389348 0

The Basics

GENOCIDE

THE BASICS

Paul R. Bartrop

Routledge
Taylor & Francis Group

LONDON AND NEW YORK

First published 2015
by Routledge
2 Park Square, Milton Park, Abingdon, Oxon OX14 4RN

and by Routledge
711 Third Avenue, New York, NY 10017

Routledge is an imprint of the Taylor & Francis Group, an informa business

© 2015 Paul R. Bartrop

The right of Paul R. Bartrop to be identified as author of this work has been asserted
by him in accordance with sections 77 and 78 of the Copyright, Designs and Patents
Act 1988.

All rights reserved. No part of this book may be reprinted or reproduced or utilised in
any form or by any electronic, mechanical, or other means, now known or hereafter
invented, including photocopying and recording, or in any information storage or
retrieval system, without permission in writing from the publishers.

Trademark notice: Product or corporate names may be trademarks or registered
trademarks, and are used only for identification and explanation without intent to
infringe.

British Library Cataloguing in Publication Data
A catalogue record for this book is available from the British Library

Library of Congress Cataloging in Publication Data
Bartrop, Paul R. (Paul Robert), 1955-
Genocide : the basics / Paul Bartrop. – 1 Edition.
pages cm
Includes bibliographical references and index.
1. Genocide. 2. Genocide–Prevention. I. Title.
HV6322.7B3734 2014
364.15'1–dc23
2014005263

ISBN: 978-0-415-81726-4 (hbk)
ISBN: 978-0-415-81725-7 (pbk)
ISBN: 978-1-315-76123-7 (ebk)

Typeset in Bembo
by Taylor & Francis Books

UNIVERSITY OF WINCHESTER

03893480 364.
151
BAR

MIX
Paper from
responsible sources
FSC
www.fsc.org   FSC® C013056

Printed and bound in Great Britain by
TJ International Ltd, Padstow, Cornwall

CONTENTS

PREFACE

Studying genocide can be complicated, challenging, and emotionally harrowing. I hope that in this short book I have managed to contextualise what genocide is, has been, and, perhaps, will cease to be in the future.

I would like to thank my dear friend and colleague Michael Dickerman (Richard Stockton College of New Jersey), who read every line of the first draft of this work. His critical comments were a boon to the writing process, and made the job of refining both a pleasure and an easy task.

The help proffered by my wife Eve Grimm, truly a woman whose price is above rubies, continues to be invaluable.

I have dedicated this work to Michael Cohen, a brilliant educator, inspiring leader, and outstanding human being, in gratitude for his friendship over many years.

Simultaneously, I have also dedicated this book to the memory of all those millions who have been the victims of genocide in our own and previous ages, in the hope that those who read it might find a way to render its subject a thing of the past forever.

One note should be mentioned: owing to the length of the work, it is impossible to include here every case of genocide, crime against humanity, war crime, or ethnic cleansing that has occurred throughout human history. With that in mind, my ambition is that readers interested in learning about other cases of genocide will be appropriately stimulated to chart their own course, based on the start given here.

INTRODUCTION
DEFINING GENOCIDE

The term "**genocide**" was coined in 1944 by Raphael Lemkin (1900–59). Born on June 24, 1900 in the rural village of Bezwodene in eastern Poland (then part of the Russian Empire), his Jewish background, coupled with a natural love of learning, saw him develop an interest in human morality and how it was to be channelled for goodness. A lawyer and legal scholar, Lemkin later became, in turn, a Polish soldier, refugee, and chief architect of what became the **international law** that made genocide a recognised crime (Bartrop 2012: 186–189).

By 1929, Lemkin had been appointed Deputy Public Prosecutor in Warsaw. In 1933, when an international conference on penal and criminal law met in Madrid in Spain, Lemkin felt that the time was ripe for him to present an idea he had been turning around in his head as a result of learning of the Ottoman Turkish destruction of the Armenians (see **Chapter 3**): an international law addressing two crimes of "barbarity" and "vandalism." The former he defined as destroying a national or religious collectivity; the latter as destroying works of culture representative of the genius of such groups. Though he had sent his paper ahead, Lemkin was prevented from attending by the Polish Minister of Justice, who saw Lemkin's work solely as a *Jewish* issue. Between 1933 and 1939, Lemkin continued to sharpen his thinking about the legal implications and ramifications of such violence against groups.

By early 1941, with **war** raging in Europe, Lemkin left Poland with the aid of friends, and made his way to the United States. He settled into a teaching position at Duke University, North Carolina, where his contacts had managed to secure an academic appointment for him at the Duke Law School.

One year later, Lemkin submitted to President Franklin Delano Roosevelt (1882–1945) a one-page proposal for an international treaty banning "vandalism and barbarity." Roosevelt responded affirmatively, but, due to the exigencies of the war itself, such work would have to come later.

At the same time, Lemkin was also working hard on his massive 674-page book *Axis Rule in Occupied Europe: Laws of Occupation, Analysis of Government, Proposals for Redress*, which would be published in 1944 by the Carnegie Endowment for International Peace in Washington, DC. Addressing the issue of Nazi atrocities against Jews, Lemkin devoted the entirety of Chapter 9 to a discussion of what he called "genocide" – a "new term and new conception for destruction of nations" (Lemkin 1944: 79) He coined the term by linking the Greek word *genos* (tribe, nation) with the Latin suffix *-cide* (killing). As he saw it, the Nazi assault in Europe was cause for a great deal of serious reflection about the state of humanity in the modern world, and on its future. Accordingly, he wrote, "New conceptions require new terms. By 'genocide' we mean the destruction of a nation or ethnic group. ... It is intended ... to signify a coordinated plan of different actions aiming at the destruction of essential foundations of life of national groups, with the aim of annihilating the groups themselves" (Lemkin 1944: 79).

After the war, Lemkin became obsessed with seeking recognition of his term from the newly established United Nations, and achieving passage of a bill banning such destruction into international law. He faced considerable difficulties, not the least of which was that he was just one man with a theory, acting in no official capacity, nor representing any agency or government.

After many bureaucratic and legal battles, on December 9, 1948 the General Assembly of the United Nations, with the support of both its Legal Committee and the Security Council, passed the Convention for the Prevention and Punishment of the Crime of Genocide. The vote was unanimous.

The initial model of the **Convention** was in large part drafted by Lemkin himself, though considerable redrafting at committee stage saw it changed noticeably from what had originally been envisaged. Article 2 of the final document embodies the definition of genocide, which was contentious both then and now:

> In the present Convention, genocide means any of the following acts committed with intent to destroy, in whole or in part, a national, ethnical, racial or religious group, as such:
>
> a) Killing members of the group;
> b) Causing serious bodily or mental harm to members of the group;
> c) Deliberately inflicting on the group conditions of life calculated to bring about its physical destruction in whole or in part;
> d) Imposing measures intended to prevent births within the group;
> e) Forcibly transferring children of the group to another group.
>
> (Totten and Bartrop 2009: 30–33)

A few key points can be made by way of a critique of the Convention and this definitive Article. First, genocide is a criminal act, which the signatories promise to "prevent" and "punish." Second, for a successful charge of genocide to be brought the notion of intent on the part of the perpetrators must be proven. Third, destruction can be "in whole" or "in part," though just how many individuals constitute "in part" is not spelled out. Fourth, four possible groups are listed as the only acceptable targets for genocide; thus if other groups of people are persecuted – for example as a result of political affiliation, social origin, cultural background, or sexual preference – these are not included within the UN's definition of genocide. Finally, killing is not the only means to commit genocide as four other activities, in which lives are not necessarily taken, are also considered.

Genocide covers many actions, though the proven intent to destroy is what really matters: if the ultimate aim is the permanent and deliberate elimination of the targeted group from the wider population, then it is genocide.

The UN definition is not all-encompassing. While including acts of destruction that are not lethal to a group, several groups were omitted that arguably should be included. These cover social and political groups; the types of actions that could be included as genocide could be widened; and the meaning of "intent" should be clarifed. The fact is that, owing to a series of compromises involving the major powers of the day, none of these proposed changes made their way into the final form the Convention agreed in 1948. Because the Convention resulted from compromise, and in spite of changing circumstances over more than six decades since it appeared, changing the Convention and its definition will probably be more difficult to achieve than it was to originally secure its passage.

The number of events throughout history that have since 1948 been termed genocide has resulted in confusion regarding what genocide should be; indeed, a full scholarship of genocide has emerged. Invariably, a great deal of genocide theory proceeds from (and all too often gets bogged down by) discussions relating to definitional matters. Where Lemkin's original conception began with the statement that genocide means "the destruction of a nation or ethnic group," other definitions diverge from this (Totten and Bartrop 2008: 101–102). Other forms of destruction that do not fit comfortably into Article 2 have led to even newer terms being developed: in addition to genocide, ideas such as **ethnocide**, politicide, democide, omnicide, gendercide, and **autogenocide**, among many others, have been formulated. While these notions are often useful in creating models to help approach specific issues, it could, however, be argued that the full scope of genocide has yet to be exhausted.

Genocide, first and foremost, is a crime – a crime of the greatest magnitude, and a major problem afflicting the very definition of modern civilisation. Whether or not we would like to admit it, genocide – and the threat of genocide – has become one of the defining features of our time.

Historically, the causes of genocide are difficult to pin down. Only with hindsight is some kind of connection visible between an event and what transpired beforehand. Whether one can ultimately arrive at a common causal denominator for all genocides is doubtful, though some features do stand out. Frequently, genocides take place in times of war. Usually, some sort of ideology is present that demonises a target group and demands its eradication. Elsewhere, times of extreme economic stress can lead to an outbreak of mass violence, while inter-communal violence can take place when there is a radical imbalance of power between those seeking destruction and their intended victims.

These factors, in themselves, do not automatically lead to genocide. Populations have to be conditioned to accept it, often over a lengthy period of time, otherwise a perpetrator regime is seen to be going too far and the population will reject its actions.

The flashpoint, or trigger, will always vary from case to case. Such incidents cannot always be predicted in advance, and, as with all historical events, there are so many variables that it is impossible to foresee how an event will resolve itself before it actually does.

It is in view of this that we need to consider the root cause behind the establishment of international legislation designed to confront genocide. In the enormous death toll of the Great War, the vast majority of those killed were military deaths: our best estimates tell us that, on average, 5,600 soldiers were killed per day, every day, for four and a quarter years. Civilians numbered only 5 per cent of all deaths in combat zones during the Great War (Bartrop 2002: 512–532).

After that conflict, the rate of civilian deaths in wartime increased enormously. By the Second World War, civilians could be calculated at 66 per cent of all war-related deaths; into the 1970s and 1980s, civilian deaths in war headed towards 80 per cent (Bartrop 2002: 512–532). The vast majority of such deaths can be put down to an accumulation of **massacres** (some pre-determined, some spontaneous) and genocide (by definition deliberate).

The chapters that follow will serve as a short narrative summary of a series of case studies of genocide, and as an introduction to some of the international implications of these case studies. In a work of this length, it is impossible to dissect all the implications of every issue within the field of genocide studies, so this volume can only stand as an elementary overview of the fundamentals of the subject.

The concept of genocide is not an easy one to understand. Because it is locked directly into a legal definition that defines the concept and forms the international legislation that makes it a crime, there is a dissenting view that any definition of genocide should be expanded in order to explain all the horrors and injustices that the world has witnessed. Starting the process that can lead to an understanding of the causes, meanings, and realities of genocide is what this book seeks to do.

DISCUSSION QUESTIONS

- Why are definitional matters of such importance for scholars of genocide?
- Is it possible to define the term "genocide" in any way other than legally?
- What are some of the key elements of the UN Convention on the Prevention and Punishment of the Crime of Genocide 1948, and why are they contentious?
- To what extent is genocide dependent upon the deliberate intent of the perpetrators? Can genocide take place where no such intent is present?

2

COLONIAL GENOCIDES

THE NATURE OF COLONIAL DESTRUCTION

Colonialism is a form of political control by one state over another, frequently characterised by the establishment of settler communities resulting in the displacement, absorption, or destruction of pre-existing indigenous populations. The process of colonisation from the sixteenth century onwards, especially that involving incursions by European states into the Americas, Asia, Africa, and Australasia, has often been typified by violent confrontation, deliberate massacre, wholesale annihilation, and, in several instances, genocide. It was largely responsible for reshaping the demographic composition of vast areas of the world's surface, and where it took hold, huge numbers of settlers from European states left their homelands to start new outgrowth communities (or to reinforce those already there). In so doing, they took over, sometimes quite brutally, land already occupied by indigenous populations. The resultant expansion of European powers saw many indigenous peoples from the lands that were taken over completely, or almost completely, wiped out – for example the Yuki of California, the Beothuks of Newfoundland, the Pallawah of Tasmania, and the Herero of Namibia, to name but a handful. Genocidal massacres were not infrequent.

It is vitally important that care is taken when employing the term "genocide" relative to colonial expansion: each and every claim must be assessed individually and on its merits. In some instances, genocide might be unequivocal; in others, despite a sudden or enormous population collapse, intent on the part of the colonisers seeking this outcome was absent. Often, diseases that arrived with the colonisers were responsible, and the deaths unanticipated. Elsewhere, lethal diseases were deliberately introduced for the purpose of wiping out a population.

In most cases, it could be said that colonial expansion saw attempts at clearing the land of indigenous populations; of forcibly assimilating the indigenous populations for racial, religious, or ethnic reasons; or of intimidating indigenous populations such that they would seek to retreat before the advance of the colonisers. The human cost was devastating and long-lasting for the indigenous populations being taken over.

The seventeenth to nineteenth centuries saw huge colonial population movements from Europe to many lands of recent European settlement, such as the United States, Canada, Australia, South Africa, New Zealand, Argentina, Brazil, and Chile. Frequently this was accompanied by massive violations of **human rights** against those who had already been living in the conquered territories. Without deliberate intent, of course, it is inaccurate to refer to an act as genocide. However, there are often occasions in the process of colonial expansion in which populations collapse where no premeditation is present. The collapse of a population occurs when a previously viable group is reduced to such a degree that the usual characteristics of a society – reproduction, habitation, and sustenance – fall to such a level that the remaining members of that society are incapable of undertaking even these fundamentals. In some cases, starvation might be the root cause of population loss; in others, it might be disease; in yet others, it might be an insufficient birth rate, perhaps exacerbated by either (or both) of the former concerns.

While starvation, disease, and a low birth rate could themselves be the product of genocidal developments, particularly in the case of indigenous societies being assailed by foreign colonisation, sometimes populations collapse when no genocidal intent is present. In the study of genocide it is crucial that the reasons for population collapse are studied, because a sudden disintegration of a population is not always attributable to genocide alone.

Disease is an important indicator when considering colonial genocide. When we speak of disease relative to genocide, we most commonly are referring to lethal epidemics that have wrought significant harm to the current or future population size of a group. The great scourges of history – such as smallpox, cholera, tuberculosis, influenza, leprosy, measles, and bubonic plague – were frequently visited upon whole societies as highly infectious viral outbreaks for which there was no immediate cure, and in which hundreds of thousands, and even millions, died. Where the study of genocide is concerned, a key issue is whether, and to what degree, these diseases are or were introduced by a perpetrator with the intention of destroying a population.

No comprehensive conclusions can be drawn on this, as circumstances have varied greatly throughout the world over the last several centuries. In some situations, there is no doubt that viral bacteria were released deliberately into a group with the intention of wiping them out. However, the vast majority of those who have died over the period in question succumbed owing to their vulnerability to microbes that accompanied encroaching groups. In North America, Australasia and the Pacific, for instance, local populations from the sixteenth century onwards had never before experienced European or Asian diseases. Often, these had wiped out large sections of local populations well before any of those from the encroaching nations had even begun their engagement with the native inhabitants. There is certainly a relationship between disease and genocide, but how far that extends is a matter that can never be taken for granted, and must always be dealt with cautiously.

THE AMERICAS

The European invasion of the Americas was accompanied by massive losses for the indigenous populations across both continents, and whole libraries have been written dealing with relations between those coming into these lands and those who were already there. In Spanish America, for instance, examples of ecclesiastical and lay cruelty often feature in accounts of the mass extermination of the native populations in the sixteenth and seventeenth centuries.

Entire islands in the Caribbean were wiped out, while whole civilisations in Central and South America sometimes fell at the hands of those known as *Conquistadores*.

The genocide of indigenous peoples throughout the Americas represents one of the greatest and most extensive human catastrophes in history. The pace and magnitude of the destruction varied from region to region over the years, but it can be safely concluded that in the two and a half centuries following Christopher Columbus's "discovery" of the Americas in 1492, probably 95 per cent of the pre-Columbian population was wiped out – by disease as well as by deliberate policy on the part of the Spanish, the French, the English, and, ultimately, by the American-born heirs of those colonising nations (Stannard 1993).

The process of colonisation was often characterised by violent confrontation, deliberate massacre, wholesale annihilation, and genocide. In North America, many indigenous peoples were completely, or almost completely, eradicated.

As an example, we can consider the Yuki people of northern California. The Yuki were an indigenous people of the Coast Range Mountains region, centred on the Eel River. Their lifestyle had been a prosperous one based on fishing and gathering the bounty of the rich forests within which they lived.

A people numbering between 10–12,000 at the time of first contact with the Americans, the Yuki population collapsed steadily in the three decades after the late 1850s (Totten and Bartrop 2008: 481–482). Increasing contact between the Yuki and incoming white settlers led to clashes, usually over property in the form of the settlers' livestock. Later violence took on an exterminatory character: settler parties would often go looking for Yuki to kill or take as prisoners; these prisoners would be taken to a Federal Indian Reservation at Round Valley, though this did nothing to stop settler depredations. Indeed, there were times when the killing went on at Round Valley itself.

Moreover, a unit of local volunteers calling themselves the Eel River Rangers, under the command of Captain Walter S. Jarboe (1827–69), was formed exclusively for the purpose of killing Yuki. Over the six-month duration of the unit's existence during 1859–60, the number of Yuki, regardless of age or sex, was reduced substantially. It has been estimated that by late 1860 only a few hundred Yuki remained, and within the next 40 years this had fallen to only a handful. The genocide of the Yuki was one of the fastest and most complete of any of those committed against Native Americans, and took the form both of settler murder and of deliberate colonial policy (Totten and Bartrop 2008: 481–482).

When considering genocide in the United States we are looking at a horrific series of cases of mass human destruction in which millions of people lost their lives. The destruction did not stop once most of the people had died or been killed; US policies of population removal, dispossession of lands, forced assimilation, and confinement to government-created reservations meant that in a vast number of cases even the survivors were denied the opportunity to retain their identity as distinct peoples.

The foundations of indigenous destruction were many, and varied from place to place. The quest for land and religious conversion, the development of concepts of racial inferiority and superiority, displacement, and population transfer undertaken in the pursuit of "progress" on the frontiers of European or American settlement – all of these had their place in the devastation of the Native Americans. Individual murders, occasional massacres, and wholesale annihilation in long-term campaigns facilitated violent destruction. That genocide of specific Native American groups took place is beyond doubt; but this must be tempered by the qualification that not all destruction or population collapse occurred as the result of deliberate intent on the part of the settlers. On those occasions where intent *can* be detected, a case for genocide might be prosecuted, but the disintegration of the Native American world was not a monolithic event and must, therefore, be examined carefully and thoroughly, with an eye to the particularity of each people, region, and time period, and without preconceived opinions.

The forced removal of the Native American peoples of the south-east of the United States presents us with one such dilemma. Can this be considered a case of genocide? In 1830, US President Andrew Jackson (1767–1845) signed the Indian Removal Act, a law ordering the compulsory relocation of Native American peoples living east of the Mississippi River to a designated territory to the west. These peoples were known as the "Five Civilised Tribes," comprising the Cherokee, Choctaw, Creek, Chickasaw, and Seminole nations. They had adapted to European ways and taken the elements most suited to improving their quality of life, while at the same time retaining their sovereign integrity and folkways. After the Indian Removal Act, however, they were forced to cede their lands to the United States and move to other territories many hundreds of miles away. The first transfer was of the Choctaw Nation: between 1831 and 1834, most members were forced westward at the point of Federal bayonets, and in appalling conditions. Because Federal expenses for removal were inadequate, there were shortages of food, unsatisfactory means of transportation, and little in the way of warm clothing or blankets. At least a quarter of the Choctaw Nation died before they reached the new Indian Territory in modern-day Oklahoma (Alvarez 2014: 139).

A similar fate befell the others. In the case of the Creeks, an experience resembling civil war broke out between supporters and opponents of removal. When eventually they were "removed," nearly a quarter of the population had died of exposure and disease. The Chickasaws suffered less on their actual journey, but perished in large numbers after their arrival owing to disease. For as long as they were able, the Seminoles managed to resist removal, and during the Seminole Wars (1835–42) made US troops pay a heavy price. Nonetheless, several thousand were eventually transferred to Indian Territory (Alvarez 2014: 137–140).

The Cherokees, the most numerous of the Five Civilised Tribes, did all they could to avoid deportation, arguing their case in the highest US tribunals including the Senate and the Supreme Court, but they, too, were forced to leave. Approximately one-quarter of the Cherokees perished between 1838 and 1839 in what became known as the "Trail of Tears." The term now stands as a generic name for the forced removal and suffering of the Five Civilised Tribes overall, during which time tens of thousands of people died as a direct result of US government actions and failures to act (Ehle 1997).

A major massacre, motivated by genocidal intent, took place less than a generation later against the Cheyenne and Arapaho peoples of Colorado. On November 29, 1864, the Third Colorado Volunteer Cavalry Regiment, under the command of Colonel John Chivington (1821–94), led an attack against a Cheyenne village at Sand Creek. The members of this unit had signed on as Indian fighters, and under Chivington's orders had rounded up small groups of Cheyenne and Arapaho for the purpose of killing them at a time to be determined later. Then, before dawn on the morning of November 29, the Third Colorado's assault group, comprising some 700 men and four howitzers, took their intended targets by complete surprise. As the Cheyenne realised what was happening, the US troops opened fire; the ensuing massacre was so horrific that some of Chivington's own men would later turn evidence against him for allowing such abhorrent acts to take place (Bartrop 2004: 194–214; Alvarez 2014: 93–100).

The soldiers were indiscriminate in their killing. Men and women were scalped, pregnant women were ripped open, children were clubbed to death, and bodies were mutilated. No prisoners were taken. Anyone who surrendered was killed immediately. The massacre continued for five miles beyond the Sand Creek campsite, and when Chivington and the Third Colorado returned to Denver they exhibited more than a hundred scalps, the gruesome booty of a death toll that may have numbered up to 200 – of whom two-thirds were women and children, and nine were chiefs (Bartrop 2004: 194–214; Alvarez 2014: 95–96).

The massacre at Sand Creek was committed by perpetrators whose actions were not only explicit, but eagerly advertised with malice before the event and with triumph after it. Moreover, it was committed by a military force raised by the government of the Colorado Territory for the express purpose of killing every Cheyenne on whom it could lay its hands. Chivington's orders came from the Governor of Colorado, John Evans (1814–97), and were endorsed by a popular clamour throughout the Territory. Sand Creek was clearly a massacre undertaken as part of a larger campaign of genocide against the Cheyenne and Arapaho, in which the objective was that none would remain alive. It was, in its purest form, an act committed with intent to destroy, in whole or in part, a national (or ethnic, or racial) group through the deliberate policy of killing its members.

At Wounded Knee Creek, South Dakota, on December 29, 1890, a massacre of Sioux took place at the hands of the US Seventh Cavalry. The massacre, which popular wisdom has preferred to label a battle, was the final confrontation in the three-century relationship on the frontier between Native Americans and expansionist whites. The remnants of the Native American peoples of the Great Plains were by then but a shadow of what they had been. In desperation, many took heart from the messianic "Ghost Dance" cult, with its promises of a reversion to the old ways in a new world. By December 28, a large group of Lakota Sioux, numbering about 350 and led by their sick and elderly chief, Big Foot (c. 1825–90), found themselves at Pine Ridge Reservation, but were ordered by the Seventh Cavalry to camp at nearby Wounded Knee Creek. The Seventh Cavalry – still smouldering from their defeat and the death of their commander General George Armstrong Custer (1839–76) at the hands of the Sioux in the Battle of Little Bighorn in 1876 – saw this as the opportunity to settle accounts. On December 29 the soldiers disarmed the Sioux men, and then conducted a thorough search of the campsite for any additional weapons.

In a tense environment, violence began as one of the Sioux men objected to his rifle being taken away. The Sioux fighters, buoyed by the idea of an invincibility that would be transmitted to them through their Ghost Dancing and the "ghost shirts" they wore, began to fight back. The ensuing struggle was so one-sided that the term "battle" is hardly appropriate. The Sioux were cut down mercilessly. Four Hotchkiss artillery pieces surrounding the camp opened fire, scything through their victims, and less than an hour later the fighting and killing had ended. Almost two-thirds of Big Foot's people were casualties – at least 200 dead and wounded were counted, though many others were not accounted for. The army lost 25 killed and 39 wounded (Totten and Bartrop 2008: 473-474).

The "battle" at Wounded Knee was a massacre of men, women and children, the last major action of its kind in the course of westward expansion for European Americans. It is thus a watershed event; henceforward, institutional discrimination would be the means employed in the process to maintain white supremacy and second-class status for Native Americans.

AUSTRALIA

The situation concerning the Aborigines of mainland Australia during the time of colonial settlement by Britain poses a number of questions relative to genocide. The most important of these is also the most straightforward: did the destruction of Aboriginal society in the century following the arrival of the First Fleet in 1788 constitute genocide? For some, the answer is an unequivocal yes; for others, less so. There was no definite state-initiated plan of mass extermination; indeed, it was frequently the case that colonial governments (on paper, at least) sought to maintain Aboriginal security in the face of settler and pastoralist encroachments, and imposed punishments (even hangings) on those found guilty of the murder of Aborigines.

Despite this, there were immense and very intensive periods of killing in the bush, accompanied by enormous population losses as a result of disease and starvation. One of these, the massacre at Warrigal Creek, in the Gippsland region of the Port Phillip District (now Victoria), was arguably the greatest single massacre of Aborigines in Australian history (Bartrop 2004: 194–214).

Early British settlement of Gippsland focuses on the life and career of Angus McMillan (1810–65). In June, 1843, McMillan led a posse of about 20 settlers – comprised of cattle owners, stockmen, and other whites in the vicinity – against a group of Kurnai whom they held responsible for the death of another of their number, Ronald Macalister. Prior to setting out, McMillan warned the party that their mission had to be carried out in utmost secrecy. A blood oath was sworn never to divulge the truth of the acts they were about to commit, as it was well known that, in December 1838, seven white men had been hanged for the murder of 28 Aborigines at Myall Creek, New South Wales (Moses 2004: dedication page).

Setting out from McMillan's property at Bushy Park, the posse found a large group of Kurnai camped beside a waterhole on Warrigal Creek. Within 20 minutes, the camp was surrounded, and, on a signal from McMillan, the men opened fire from all directions. Kurnai were shot in the camp, as they ran, after they had jumped into the waterhole, and when they put their heads up for breath. In less than half an hour, the massacre was complete; by all subsequent accounts, up to 150 were murdered (Bartrop 2004: 194–214; Gardner 1990).

In the weeks that followed, more were killed, possibly to a figure of 450. McMillan, the "scourge of the Kurnai," won Gippsland for white settlement through violence and mass murder, and, by the late 1850s, the number of Aborigines had been slashed, by one estimate, to under 100 (from a pre-contact population of about 3,000). After this, McMillan was hailed as a hero and respected father figure in the colony. Appointed a Justice of the Peace and elected to the Victorian Legislative Assembly, he later became – ironically – an official Protector of Aborigines (Gardner 1990).

Events such as the massacre at Warrigal Creek took place all over Australia, the result leading to the effective destruction of Aboriginal society by European settlement during the nineteenth century.

In the colony of Queensland, a policy of shooting at Aborigines in the rural regions, with the intention of killing them, was known by the euphemism of "dispersal." This allowed for the prospect of shooting *in the direction of* Aborigines so that they might take fright and run away, but, in reality, it transpired that large numbers of Aborigines were killed deliberately. For the most part, "dispersals" were undertaken by troopers of the Queensland Native Mounted Police, a force comprised of Murri men recruited from various parts of the colony and commanded by white officers. The policy of "dispersal" came under the spotlight in 1861 when a government Select Committee looked into the matter. It was openly acknowledged that "dispersing" equated with shooting, and that deaths were frequently caused through indiscriminate hunting down of whole groups without any recognition of individual difference. It was held that there was "no other way" to remove Aborigines from the path of European settlement than by shooting at them. By the end of the process, thousands had been gunned down and Queensland had been opened up for white pastoral settlement (Reynolds 2001: 99–118).

The indigenous peoples of the island of Tasmania, the Pallawah, are of a different (and largely unknown) background to those of mainland Australia. In 1803, a convict colony was established near modern-day Hobart, after which Aboriginal life was never to be the same again. Along with the convicts came sealers and whalers, pastoralists and town-dwellers, as the full range of early nineteenth century British society descended on the indigenous inhabitants like a tidal wave.

Full-scale war between the Aborigines and the whites broke out in 1829 and lasted until 1831, with the Aborigines waging a guerrilla campaign that was so successful that, at one point, Hobart Town seemed to be in danger of evacuation. The so-called Black War was to claim many lives on both sides. In late 1830, in order to bring the violence to an end, 2,200 men, including 500 troops, formed a line – "the Black Line" – and marched across the island in a quest to capture as many Aborigines as possible. It was a dismal and expensive failure. In the mid-1830s, a new initiative was introduced: British conciliation with the Aborigines, with the intention of persuading them to come into the white-settled areas voluntarily. By 1835, most had done so.

The government had earlier established a mission station and settlement, Wybalenna, on nearby Flinders Island, where the 123 remnants of the Pallawah were now relocated. Within sight of the Tasmanian mainland, but separated by distance in space and time from the free lives they once enjoyed, the devastated population expired steadily, some by disease, others from despair. In 1869, the last full-blooded male Aborigine, William Lanne (also known as King Billy) (c. 1835–March 3, 1869), died; in 1876, the last full-blooded female, Truggernanna (c. 1812–76), also died. This population collapse was as complete as any that had taken place elsewhere, and probably more than most. The extent to which this can be described as genocide, however, has been hotly debated in Australian scholarship, with positions both for and against argued with increasing vehemence in the years following the centenary of Truggernanna's death (Ryan 1981; Reynolds 2001: 67–96).

Where genocide is concerned in the context of Australian colonialism, it must be understood against two essential facts. In the first place, there was no unified stance on Aborigines throughout the century, as the Australian continent was divided into six separate British colonies until Federation in 1901. Secondly, no government at any time displayed the necessary intent, in word or in deed, which would prove the existence of a genocidal policy. This is no way mitigates the catastrophe that destroyed the Aborigines, but neither does history show conclusively that the tragedy was the result of what might be termed genocide.

In the twentieth century, however, an official Australian government policy did constitute genocide, as defined under the 1948 UN Genocide Convention, whose Article 2(e) refers to the forcible transfer of children from a group to another group for the purpose of permanently transforming the group's identity. In Australia, this translated to the compulsory permanent removal of children of part-Aboriginal descent from their parents and subsequent place-ment with non-Aboriginal parents. The intention was that they would grow to maturity as white children, marry white partners, and that, as a result, over time all traces of Aboriginality would be "bred out" (Reynolds 2001: 163–171).

The policy was prompted by a belief, widespread in many areas of the Australian bureaucracy, that while the full-blooded Aboriginal population was destined to die out completely, those of mixed descent, if permitted to grow in numbers to hundreds of thousands or even a million, would create a problem. Restricting breeding opportunities between people of mixed descent thus became the preferred approach to dealing with the issue; the best way to achieve this, it was felt, was to separate mixed-descent Aborigines from each other, and to expose them only to white options for their future lives.

This tactic was to last in various forms until the 1970s. It deci-mated at least two generations of Aborigines of mixed descent, and in a 1997 Commonwealth report into the whole issue – undertaken by the Human Rights and Equal Opportunity Commission – the allegation of genocide was for the first time raised in an official capacity. The inquiry concluded that a case for genocide could be made (Totten and Bartrop 2008: 51).

CANADA

To a large degree, Canada was spared much of the violence com-mitted against Native Americans in the United States. This is not to say that the First Nations (as they are termed) escaped **persecution**, dispossession, or measures introduced to weaken their position as European settlement took place. Indeed, the Beothuks of Newfoundland were completely destroyed (as a result of starvation, disease, and settler perpetrated murder), and the situation in other parts of Maritime Canada were little better; large-scale population collapse was widespread among certain peoples, such as the Miqmaq.

The indigenous people of Newfoundland, the Beothuks, num-bered anywhere between 500 and 2,000 at the time of their first European contact in the sixteenth century, though the higher figure is the more likely. The population collapsed steadily, however, after the middle of the eighteenth century. It has been estimated that by 1823 the Beothuk population had been reduced by 96 per cent of its approximate total at first contact. The pitiable few Beothuks left by the end of the decade could probably be counted on the fingers of two hands, if they could be found (Marshall 1998).

The major reasons behind the demise of the Beothuk population can be attributed to settler depredations and murders, a decline in Beothuk hunting areas, kidnapping of Beothuk women and a consequent decline in reproductive potential, and – above all – diseases, particularly tuberculosis.

Yet for all that, the British colonial government did not pursue a policy aimed at their destruction. In 1769 there was, instead, a clear statement, through a proclamation from Governor John Byron (1723–86), that the murder of Beothuks was a capital crime, and during the first two decades of the nineteenth century – by which time it was far too late – there were a number of official attempts undertaken to rescue the last Beothuks from what was regarded as an inevitable fate.

In June, 1829, a young Beothuk woman, Shanawdithit (c. 1803–29), died of tuberculosis in St John's; she is generally regarded as "the last Beothuk." Close examination of the fate of the Beothuk people indicates that it was not as a result of genocide that they became extinct. Although many were murdered by settler encroachment, other factors – such as a collapse in the availability of food sources, disease, and a withdrawal of the Beothuk from contact with the whites to areas from which they could not be helped – were responsible for the Beothuks' demise.

The first sweeping legislation covering Canada's First Nations peoples came in 1850, with the passage of the Statute for Lower Canada where the term "Indian" was first defined legally. In 1870, an Act to Encourage the Gradual Civilisation of the Indian Tribes in the Province and to Amend the Laws Respecting Indians was passed. The Act encouraged assimilation by permitting male Indians to "enfranchise" by renouncing their First Nations status and living as Europeans did.

The situation regarding those of mixed descent, as in Australia, presented problems for successive white governments, but in Canada the affected population fought back. The Métis people, descended from the mixture of both First Nations (for example Cree, Ojibway, and Assiniboine) and European settlers (primarily French, but also English), formed themselves into what they self-identified as a "New People." Those killed in direct military clashes with British and Canadian troops, culminating in the Red River Resistance of 1870 and the North-West Rebellion of 1885, were few in number, but Canada's treatment of the Métis from the late nineteenth century onwards saw the attempted destruction of their distinctive identity using non-genocidal means (Peterson and Brown 2001).

As Canada expanded westward, and first British then Canadian military might conquered the Métis in battle in a quest to expropriate land, the Métis were forced to defend themselves against dispossession, dispersal, and military occupation. Neither the Métis nor the Canadians sought to embrace each other into the nation-building process; the Métis were committed to a sense of their own distinctive peoplehood, and were thoroughly alienated from a Canadian national ethos. The Canadians, for their part, discouraged the maintenance of a separate Métis identity and adopted measures intended to diminish it. Although many federal and provincial measures were enacted throughout the twentieth century regarding Métis welfare, education, health, and social position, little was done to safeguard or recognise their distinctiveness as a founding people of the Canadian Confederation. It was not until 1982 that the Métis Nation was acknowledged as an Aboriginal People of Canada, though by then a great deal of damage to Métis distinctiveness had already been done.

Arguments abound concerning Canada's treatment of its First Nations populations. Some assert that Canada's first Prime Minister, Sir John A. MacDonald (1815–91) pursued a policy of enforced starvation in order to make way for the western expansion of European settlers. Others argue that, under the treaty system, native leaders were required to surrender **sovereignty** to the Crown, a measure intended to destroy the identity of the First Nations through cultural assimilation.

The most damning accusations refer to the Indian residential schools system, a national education scheme created in 1876. It has been estimated that about 150,000 First Nations children passed through the residential schools. Enormous harm was done to these children by removing them from their families, depriving them of their ancestral languages, and exposing many of them to physical and sexual abuse. In this, their experiences were not unlike the Aboriginal children in Australia, who were placed in residential homes before being sent out to white families. The difference, however, is that in Canada there was no attempt at what the Australians termed "biological absorption," simply a major cultural transformation that would see Indian children grow up not knowing anything about their culture or folkways (Milloy 1999).

While it cannot be argued successfully as a whole that successive Canadian governments, in their capacity as colonisers, engaged in genocide against the First Nations as policy, it can certainly be argued that an enormous amount of cultural destruction took place as the country was being won for white settlement.

NAMIBIA

The German assault against the Herero people in 1904–7, during Germany's colonial possession of South-West Africa (now Namibia), can be termed the first true instance of genocide in the twentieth century. During this time, the destruction of up to 80 per cent of the total population took place. At least 50 per cent of the Nama, or "Hottentot," population were also wiped out at this time (Sarkin 2010: 136–142).

In late 1903, Herero leaders learned of a proposal the Germans were considering that would see the construction of a railway line through Herero territory, and the consequent concentration in reservations of Herero living there. In response, in January 1904, the Herero rebelled with the intention of driving the Germans out. At this time, according to the best estimates, the Herero numbered some 80,000 (Drechsler 1980: 17).

After a German counterattack, reinforcement, and a widespread campaign of annihilation and displacement that forced huge numbers of Herero of both sexes and all ages into the Omaheke Desert, tens of thousands perished. The situation was exacerbated by the policy of German General Lothar von Trotha (1848–1920), who ordered that all waterholes be located and poisoned in advance of the arrival of those Herero who might have survived the desert (Dreschler 1980: 156–157; Sarkin 2010: 114–116).

The roots of the genocide can be found in several areas. These include colonialism, Christian missionising, economic self-interest, slave labour, militarism, nationalism, and **racism**.

In 1883, Franz Adolf Eduard Lüderitz (1834–86), a German businessman and merchant, purchased a strip of land from the Nama people at what would later be called Lüderitzbucht (Lüderitz Bay). A small settlement was established there, and within a year Lüderitz managed to have the area declared a protectorate of the German government. By 1885 a treaty of protection against the neighbouring tribes was signed between the Herero chief Kamaharero (1820–90) and the then-colonial governor Heinrich Ernst Göring (1839–1913), father of the later Nazi leader, Hermann Göring (1893–1946).

As the colony grew, Göring was replaced by Theodor Leutwein (1849–1921), whose policies included unsuccessful attempts to mediate between the German colonists and the native peoples. Continuous tribal conflict that threatened the safety and economic potential of the German colony saw Germany send *Schutztruppe* ("Protection Troops") to pacify the area. Increasingly, however, the Germans exploited the native labourers (often transforming them into *de facto* slaves), **raped** their women, and encroached onto their lands without compensation.

In 1903, the Nama people, under the leadership of Hendrik Witbooi (c. 1830–1905), rose in revolt, and the following year the Herero joined them in increasingly larger numbers because of the continuing loss of their lands to the German settlers. An attack that same year resulted in the death of 150 Germans and found Leutwein unable to quell the rebellion. Under the circumstances, he was forced to request reinforcements from Germany. On June 11, 1904, General Lothar von Trotha arrived with 14,000 troops. An avowed racist, von Trotha saw the only military solution as one of extermination and annihilation, and on October 1, 1904 he issued his infamous *Vernichtungsbefehl* ("Extermination Order") (Dreschler 1980: 156–157).

This was brought to fruition at the Battle of Waterberg on August 11–12, 1904, when von Trotha defeated 5,000 Herero fighters using a tactic of advancing on three sides leaving the only escape route into the Omaheke Desert – where the remaining fighters and their families would die of exposure and lack of food and water

(Bridgman 1981: 111–131). Some of those who managed to survive the desert experience escaped to British Bechuanaland. Others survived only to be captured and killed, without mercy, on von Trotha's direct orders.

On April 22, 1905, von Trotha issued orders, in unequivocal terms, that the Nama should surrender or face immediate extermination if found at large in German-controlled areas. Very soon, over half the Nama – about 10,000 – were killed (Bridgman 1981: 165).

Von Trotha was indeed successful in meeting the terms of his orders to put down the uprising in South-West Africa, but his means of doing so generated criticism both within Germany and outside of it. In 1907, his orders were cancelled, a gesture robbed of much of its meaning owing to his ferocious success in putting down the rebellions.

However, it was primarily under both his and Leutwein's successor, Governor General Friedrich von Lindequist (1862–1945), that stage two of the genocide would take place with the implementation and institution of *Konzentrationslager* ("concentration camps") and *Arbeitslager* ("work camps"). Together, these might have more appropriately been termed *Vernichtungslager*, or "death camps." One location, which many have indeed since termed a death camp, was located at Shark Island, adjacent to Lüderitz. Shark Island prisoners were used as forced labour on infrastructure projects such as railroad construction and the development of the nearby harbour. Most prisoners sent to Shark Island died, though the population was replenished constantly. The main reasons for death included diseases such as typhoid, malnutrition, extreme overwork, and constant brutality. Conditions were appalling: an official report in 1908 identified a mortality rate of well over 40 per cent across the camp system (Sarkin 2010: 136–142). While this mainly hit Herero who were incarcerated, many of the Nama also succumbed.

By the time the uprising was considered to be over, the Herero and Nama populations had effectively been destroyed by military action, starvation and thirst, disease, and by overwork in the concentration and labour camps. Evidence exists of medical experiments having been carried out (Sarkin 2010: 244), and of sexual crimes having been committed against Herero women (Sarkin 2010: 163). In 1911, when a count was made of the surviving Herero, only about 15,000 could be found, and even fewer of the

Nama (Drechsler 1980: 214). The vast majority of the rest had been killed, either directly or indirectly, by German forces over the preceding half-dozen years, though the majority of the killing had taken place during the period 1904–5.

THE IMPACT OF COLONIALISM

Colonialism in the form of the establishment of settler communities results in the displacement, absorption, or destruction of pre-existing indigenous communities. In the histories outlined here, large numbers of settlers left their original homes, usually in Europe, to start new communities or to join earlier pioneers. Inevitably, they took over land already occupied by native inhabitants. Genocidal massacres of the latter were not infrequent, and ongoing oppression or neglect has in numerous cases persisted down to the present day. Colonialism also led to the suppression of local languages, religions, and folkways: settler-colonists were always on the lookout for ways to consolidate their dominance and head off what they perceived as threats to the expansion of "their" territory in the new land. For the native populations being taken over, the human cost was devastating and long-lasting, and the injury done to their sense of identity and self-worth has in many cases yet to be resolved.

It must be reiterated, however, that care must be employed when referring to this destruction as genocide. It is impossible to generalise when discussing the cumulative effect of five centuries, several continents, numerous colonising nations, multiple affected communities, and an enormous array of government initiatives and policies. It is tempting when accounting for huge population collapses, such as those that have accompanied colonial expansion, to reach for the label of "genocide" as a way of explaining the losses. This, however, is very far from a useful strategy, given the colossal variations that must be considered.

DISCUSSION QUESTIONS

- Does the American policy of forced removal, under the Indian Removal Act 1830, constitute an act of genocide? If not, how else might it be classified?
- Was the Black War in Tasmania a genocidal conflict?

- Can the destruction of Australian Aboriginal society in the century following 1788 satisfactorily be described as a case of genocide? Why/why not?
- In what ways can colonisation into the Americas and Australia be classed as genocidal in nature?
- Was the conflict between the Germans and the Herero in South-West Africa genocidal, or just a new form of warfare?

3

THE CHRISTIANS OF THE OTTOMAN EMPIRE

THE FIRST MODERN GENOCIDE

The genocide of the Christians of the Ottoman Empire is generally acknowledged as the first "modern" genocide. Why "modern"? Because it occurred during the twentieth century, certainly, but also because it was the first time that genocide took place as the direct result of a stated ideology in which the deliberate annihilation of an entire people was both enunciated as a policy goal and carried through by the forces of the state acting in unison.

The issues involved in studying this genocide penetrate to the core of our understanding of genocide; we see **intentionality**, motive, justification, policy execution, denial, and **war crimes** trials. It also considers the notion of war as a catalyst for genocidal mass murder.

Genocide was committed against the Christian populations of the Ottoman Empire by the regime of the Committee of Union and Progress (*Ittihad ve Terakki Jemyeti*), also known as the "Young Turks," in the period following April 24, 1915. According to most accounts, at least one million – though, on the balance of probabilities, closer to 1.5 million – Armenians were slaughtered as a direct result of deliberate Turkish policies seeking their permanent eradication. At least 350,000 Greeks were murdered, as were approximately 275,000 Assyrians. In all cases, their deaths were caused by the Turks and their Kurdish collaborators (Totten and Bartrop 2008: 19, 25–26, 337).

ARMENIANS

The "Armenian Question" was a term given to describe the issue of how to bring about reforms in the condition of the Armenian population of the Ottoman Empire during the reign of Sultan Abdul Hamid II (1842–1918; reigned 1876–1909). In the latter part of the nineteenth century, the Ottoman reform movement known as *Tanzimat* attempted to restructure society on constitutional and social lines, trying to bring the Empire closer to modern European standards. The Ottoman Armenians, encouraged by this, hoped that an alteration to their status as second-class citizens might follow; consequently, a number of petitions were sent to the office of the Grand Vizier (Prime Minister) in Constantinople requesting protection from Turkish violence and ill-treatment in the provinces. Such requests were viewed by Abdul Hamid as an affront to his authority. As the question of how to treat the Armenians (and, by extension, other non-Muslim minorities within the Ottoman Empire) began to attract the attention of Europe's Christian nations, the Sultan's thoughts turned to the most efficient way of solving the "Armenian Question." His decision, by 1894, was that the only viable way of solving it would be for the Armenians to be brought to heel – and, to impart a lesson, to do so in the most brutal way possible.

Accordingly, massacres were carried out against Armenians between 1894 and 1896, with the worst occurring in 1895. Estimates of numbers killed range widely, from 100,000 to 300,000, with thousands more maimed or rendered homeless (Charny 1999: 287). Most of those killed were men; the killings took place in open areas in full sight of the community, and were designed to intimidate the Armenian population rather than cause its wholesale destruction. In a complex situation, the main explanation for the massacres lay in the Sultan's desire to check the growth of Armenian nationalism and any calls for reform that would give the Armenians a greater say in imperial affairs. It was clear also that the actions were an attempt to quash all talk of Armenian autonomy (or, worse still, independence).

These "Hamidian Massacres" (so called after the Sultan) started in mid-1894 in the region of Sasun, in southern Armenia. They spread throughout 1895, and showed that the Sultan's government had dramatically intensified the nature of anti-Armenian persecution. The massacres were thus genocidal in effect (particularly in certain regions), though not genocidal in intent – the preference being to intimidate and terrorise the Armenian population rather than to destroy them. Vast numbers of Armenians fled the country, and thousands of others were forcibly converted to Islam. In view of the ferocity of the massacres, Abdul Hamid II was nicknamed the "Red Sultan," or "Bloody Abdul," and the massacres were named after him as a way of distinguishing these actions from the later (and much more extensive) measures of 1915. They served to condition the Turkish population to accept the genocide that was undertaken from 1915 onwards, and must be seen as physical and psychological precursors to that event.

As the size of the Ottoman Empire shrank during the nineteenth and early twentieth centuries, conditions deteriorated for the Christian minority populations, and they, along with the Sultanate itself, became scapegoats for the Empire's deterioration. With the weakening of the Sultan's authority and respectability, a militant group of Turkish nationalists calling themselves the "Young Turks" (more formally the Committee of Union and Progress) launched a revolution in 1908. Their goal was to create a modern, revitalised, pan-Turkic Empire that would stretch all the way to Central Asia, for which the revivified Turkish state would need to be modernised. To achieve this, the Young Turks saw that the state would have to become militarised, industrialised, and much more nationalistic. Led by the triumvirate of Minister of the Interior Mehmet Talaat (1874–1921), Minister of War Ismail Enver (1881–1922), and Minister of the Navy Ahmed Djemal (1872–1922), the new regime instituted a plan that would see an "inclusive–exclusive" approach to the Empire's future. This would leave out the Christian Armenians, Assyrians, and Greeks, fulfilling a strategy that would transform the multicultural Ottoman society into a much more homogeneous Turkish and Islamic one.

The result saw a new round of anti-Armenian massacres in 1909, in the region surrounding the city of Adana. These were largely the result of civil strife between the supporters of the Sultan and the

Young Turk reformers, in which the Armenians appeared to be scapegoats for both sides. The Adana massacres claimed possibly up to 30,000 victims (Charny 1999: 47).

In order to justify such measures, an ideological dimension was also required so that the elites of Ottoman society could be persuaded of the need to act against the Armenian "enemy." While there were a number of ideologues with various degrees of potency, two stand out.

Ziya Gökalp (1876–1924) was a sociologist and poet who became active in Turkish nationalist agitation during the last days of the Sultanate. He was influential in redefining the meaning of Turkish nationalism, rejecting the alternatives of Ottomanism and Islamism, and instead advocating the "Turkification" of the Empire through the imposition of Turkish language and culture onto the entire population. He also developed the notions of Pan-Turkism and Turanism, with the intention of strengthening Turkey and expanding the Empire to the east – away from Europe, and into Western and Central Asia (Suny, Göçek and Naimark 2011: 33).

Dr Mehemed Nazim (1865–1926), unlike Gökalp, rose to become one of the chief ideologues of the Young Turk party, and a leading member of the inner executive of its radical wing. Nazim served as an *éminence grise* within the party, building a strong power base as one of the key supporters of Talaat. A passionate Turkish nationalist, he was in the forefront of moves to Turkify the Empire through forced assimilation, **expulsion**, or, where necessary, the killing of non-Turkish elements of the population. Nazim's greatest acrimony was reserved for the Armenians. In February, 1915 – two months before the Armenian Genocide broke out – he declared that a new **pogrom** should take place against them which would result in their complete annihilation. One of the positions for which Nazim subsequently became infamous, which he asserted during a Young Turk Central Committee meeting, was that Armenian children should not be spared but rather killed along with the adults, lest they grow up seeking revenge against the Turks (Graber 1996: 87–89).

The year 1915 saw a massive military defeat for Turkey at the hands of the Russians at the Battle of Sarikamish (December 22, 1914 to January 17, 1915) in the Caucasus Mountains; further defeats in Egypt and Sinai during February; and a difficult campaign against Russian and Russian-Armenian troops in Persia during April. When, on April 25, 1915, British, French, Indian, Australian and New Zealand (ANZAC), and Newfoundland troops landed on the Gallipoli Peninsula, the Young Turk leadership was thrown into immediate panic. The regime – indeed, the Empire – was seen to be in dire peril. Just a few days earlier, on April 20, Armenian resistance began in the city of Van, motivated by fears of deportation and certain death.

Under these tumultuous wartime conditions, the Young Turk government, feeling besieged and looking once more for a scapegoat, responded swiftly and forcefully. It implemented confidential plans that had been formulated in secret party meetings several months earlier. On the night of April 24, 1915 – a date commemorated to this day as the Armenian day of genocide remembrance – some 250 Armenian leaders in Constantinople were arrested. Most would be murdered soon after their arrest, in an action that precipitated the genocide to follow. With these measures in train – and at a time when the Turkish military forces were waging war against the Russians in the north-east and the British, French and ANZAC forces at Gallipoli – scarce military resources were diverted to the campaign of murdering the Armenian and other Christian populations. These measures were far more extensive than any previous massacres, and saw all the relevant agencies of government directed towards the singular aim of totally destroying the Armenian population.

That the genocide took place under cover of war was more than just a coincidence; the war was in reality a crucial part of the genocide's success. By conducting deportations of Armenians to places far off the beaten track, forcing many victims (primarily women and children, including babies) into under-populated regions of the Empire, the Turks were able to exploit the war situation for the purpose of achieving their genocidal aims. Technology, in the form of modern telecommunications and transportation, was employed in order to coordinate the killing activities and speed up the process, while other minorities that were supportive of the Turks' aims, in particular some Kurdish and Arab allies, assisted in carrying out the murders.

Most of those who died were the victims of heat, starvation and thirst, exposure, disease, and incessant brutality at the hands of their captors. The population was subjected to massacre, deportation, dismemberment, torture, and other atrocities. Whole cities were depopulated, and, when not killed outright, the inhabitants were expelled to their deaths. Victims were also the targets of marauding gangs of soldiers, informal militia groups, and local tribesmen that engaged in robbery, rape, and torture. By October 1915, cattle cars had been introduced in order to ship thousands of Armenians into the desert.

On May 27, 1915 the Ottoman parliament had passed the Tehcir (or "displacement") Law. Although its text did not make specific mention of the Armenians, it was one of those statutes which genocidal regimes frequently adopt that use euphemism. The law's unspecified reality saw it directed against the Armenian and Assyrian populations, leading to the deportation of all Armenians from central and eastern Anatolia. At most, they were given one- or two-days' notice; in a majority of cases, they were denied the opportunity to take their possessions with them. Most were deported into the Syrian Desert where, for many, the termination point was a mass-murder site in the natural cave formations at Dier-ez-Zor.

The Tehcir Law was ostensibly a temporary measure. It expired on February 8, 1916, but by that stage events had overtaken it. After its expiration the deportations and massacres continued so, on September 13, 1915, the Ottoman parliament passed the Temporary Law of Expropriation and Confiscation, stating that all property belonging to Armenians, including land, livestock, and homes, was to be confiscated by the state. In reality, mobs and corrupt officials frequently moved in ahead of the state authorities and simply removed what they wanted.

The eventual result of all the measures combined – deportation, hunger, thirst, brutality, shooting, and the like – was a loss of life, in a relatively short space of time, of what had hitherto been unimagined proportions. The worst of the killing was over within about 18 months, but this was only because the ferocity of the Turks' campaign led to a shortage of potential victims. This did not, however, stop the killing, and Armenian and other communities in various parts of the Empire, where they could be found, continued to be attacked through to the early 1920s.

Over time, the Armenian experience became known as the "Forgotten Genocide," due largely to two factors: first, the ongoing denial by successive Turkish governments, down to the present day, that genocide ever took place; and second, that the Armenian Genocide was eclipsed in both numbers killed and by other events of the twentieth century, particularly the Second World War and the Holocaust (Suny *et al.* 2011; Akçam 2012).

This is not to say, however, that there was ignorance of what had happened. Indeed, throughout the experience and beyond, a vast amount of evidence of the atrocities being committed found its way to the West, and was extensively publicised while it was in progress. As one example, we can consider Viscount James Bryce (1838–1922), a British intellectual, ambassador, and politician who had an authoritative knowledge of the Armenian Genocide. His lengthy association with Armenia began in the 1870s, and in 1904 he became active in the International Pro-Armenia Movement, an organisation established to raise consciousness about the need to do something to assist the Armenians owing to the Hamidian Massacres and their aftermath.

In 1915, the British government assigned Lord Bryce the task of gathering whatever could be found on the Armenian Genocide as it was developing. Taking advantage of the fact that the United States was at that time still a neutral power, he tapped into contacts he had at the US Department of State, who forwarded him American dispatches coming from Constantinople. These, together with other documents, he edited into a government "Blue Book," or official documentary collection. It was a devastating indictment of the extermination of the Armenian people at the hands of the Young Turk regime (Bryce and Toynbee 2005).

Lord Bryce's collection was published, and then presented to the British parliament by the Foreign Secretary, Viscount Grey of Fallodon (1862–1933). Bryce's hard work in finding as many relevant documents as possible influenced the British government's subsequent policy towards the Young Turk regime, and he was remembered and recognised for his efforts on behalf of the Armenian people.

In like manner, the United States Ambassador to the Ottoman Empire between 1913 and 1916, Henry Morgenthau, Sr. (1856–1946), also worked hard to draw attention to the Armenian Genocide while it was taking place. From 1915 onwards, Morgenthau found himself reporting on the situation and sending dispatches back to

Washington in a constant flow of detailed information about the unfolding genocide. This was often told in the most graphic language. His consuls in the provinces collected accounts of – and sometimes witnessed – horrifying Turkish actions, which they relayed to Morgenthau, while his own dealings with the Young Turk leaders, in particular Talaat, left no room for doubt that the total annihilation of the Armenian people was the ultimate goal.

Morgenthau's descriptions vividly exposed, in no-nonsense language, the nature and extent of Turkish measures against the Armenian people, and the experience left him exhausted and dispirited. He returned to the United States in 1916. In 1918, with State Department approval and the encouragement of President Woodrow Wilson (1856–1924), he published a memoir of his ambassadorship, *Ambassador Morgenthau's Story*, which brought to a wide reading audience the devastation wrought by the Turks on the Armenian people during 1915–16.

Finally, attention can be directed towards a third figure who tried to make a difference, a German pacifist named Armin Wegner (1886–1978). Wegner enlisted in the German army in 1914 as an officer in the medical corps, and in April 1915 was transferred to the Ottoman Empire as part of Germany's commitment to its Turkish ally. Wegner's first period of extended leave was between July and August 1915, and during that time he took it upon himself to investigate the rumours he had heard about large-scale killings of Armenians throughout the Empire. He began to travel extensively, looking for ways to chronicle what he saw (Balakian 2003: 258–259).

Disregarding orders from both the Germans and the Turks not to divulge the things he had witnessed, Wegner collected both written and visual evidence of the deportations and killings. His photographic collection captured a vast array of images documenting the Armenian Genocide, and the archive he created remains to this day a major resource confirming the genocide's reality. As his activities were illegal, however, he was forced to smuggle his material back to Germany secretly; upon being exposed for his activities, he was ultimately transferred back to Germany in disgrace.

After the First World War, he devoted himself to exposing the truth about the Armenian Genocide, and in 1919 he published an "Open Letter to President Wilson," calling for the creation of the independent Armenian state that had been promised at the Treaty of Versailles. He protested against the atrocities still at that time being committed against the Armenians, and tried to draw general attention to their ongoing plight.

PONTIC AND ANATOLIAN GREEKS

At the same time as the Armenian Genocide was taking place, the Young Turks also carried out genocides against two other Christian peoples in the Empire: the Pontic and Anatolian Greeks, and the Assyrians. As with the Armenian Genocide, a large proportion of the fatalities occurred as a result of death marches from their homelands into the Syrian Desert.

Prior to 1914, Greeks living in the Ottoman Empire were focused in the region known as Asia Minor (especially in and around Smyrna), and north-eastern and north-central Anatolia, in the area known as the Pontus (along the south-eastern shores of the Black Sea and the highlands of the interior).

An ethnically Greek population, traditionally living in the Pontus region, has maintained a continuous presence in the area for the past three millennia. Between 1914 and 1923, in a campaign reminiscent of the Armenian (and, as we will see, the Assyrian) experience that was taking place at the same time, the Pontic Greeks suffered innumerable cruelties at the hands of the Turks. An estimated 353,000 died, many on forced marches through Anatolia and the Syrian Desert (Totten and Bartrop 2008: 337).

When the Armenian Genocide began in 1915, persecutions of Pontic Greeks, which had already started in 1914, increased dramatically. Greek businesses were boycotted at government order, and, proceeding from the justification that the southern Black Sea coast was vulnerable to Russian attack (using the same rationale regarding vulnerability in the Caucasus that led to the Armenian deportations), the government ordered mass deportations of Pontic Greeks to the south, far away from their ancestral lands.

The city of Trebizond (now Trabzon), located on the Black Sea coast, was the site of one of the key battles between the Ottoman and Russian armies during the Caucasus Campaign of the First World War. In April 1916, the city was captured by Russians, who permitted the area to be governed by local leaders. Many Pontic Greeks believed that the Russian presence would last, and that the region would become an autonomous state within the Russian Empire – perhaps even a Republic of Trebizond.

When the province was restored to Turkish control in early 1918 as a result of the Russian Revolution, many Pontic Greeks left Trebizond with the departing Russians. It was then that the entire area became a major killing ground of Armenians.

The destruction of the Pontic Greeks, and the forcible deportation that followed, had but a single planned outcome: the removal of all Greeks from Turkey. Ultimately, the Turkish campaign was successful in that it destroyed forever the ancient Anatolian Greek community. Those who survived were exiled: the largest surviving Greek community, centred on the city of Smyrna, was literally pushed into the sea in 1922, with the city razed and thousands killed by the advancing Turkish Nationalist army (Milton 2008).

ASSYRIANS

The Assyrian Genocide, or *Seyfo*, took place at the hands of the Young Turks alongside the genocides of the Armenians and Greeks during and after the First World War.

An ancient people inhabiting modern-day south-eastern Iraq and north-western Iran, the Assyrians refer to their experience as having taken place between 1915 and 1918. A large proportion of the Assyrian deaths occurred as a result of death marches into the Syrian Desert, though many were also killed in their own towns and villages.

The Assyrians were subjected to massacre, deportation, dismemberment, torture, and other atrocities. Whole cities were depopulated, and, when not killed outright, the inhabitants were sent on the aforementioned death marches. By the time of the Paris Peace Conference in 1919, estimates of approximately 250,000 were given as the total number of deaths caused by the Turks and their Kurdish collaborators (Travis 2010: 262).

By way of example, we can consider one important location, the south-eastern Turkish city of Urfa, about 50 miles east of the Euphrates River. At the start of the First World War, Urfa was home to a highly mixed population of Muslims, Armenians, and Assyrians. In 1915 and 1916 the Young Turks attacked the city's Armenian and Assyrian population, resulting in a much reduced population for Urfa consisting only of Muslims. And this, it must be emphasised, was but one of hundreds of communities throughout the Empire that suffered as a result of deliberate policies of deportation that resulted in mass death.

Given that the *Seyfo* took place simultaneously with the Armenian and Greek Genocides, it has to a large extent been engulfed by the other two within the general understanding of the Ottoman genocides, of which more will be said on the following pages.

CONTROVERSIES

One of the major factors contributing toward the Turkish campaign against its Christian minorities was its pre-war commitment to the "Turkification" of the Empire. Accompanying this was an Islamic incentive, whereby the Turkish national dimension could be wedded to a Muslim revival of the Caliphate (that is, the most supreme form of Islamic state). Accordingly, on October 11, 1914, Sultan Mehmet V (1844–1918; reigned 1909–18) declared *jihad* against all Christians living in the Empire. This call to holy war was reaffirmed on November 14, 1914 by the Sheikh al-Islam (the Empire's most senior Islamic cleric).

Of interest is that this did not extend to all infidels. It was specifically directed at Christians, and did not apply to the Empire's other main minority religion, the Jewish population. This is not to say that Jews were left completely alone: just as it was for the Armenians in advance of the Russian offensive in 1915, so it was also that the entire Jewish population of Tel Aviv and Jaffa (in the region that was soon to be known as Palestine) was forcibly deported on April 6, 1917 as British and ANZAC troops pressed forward their attack. Although Muslim evacuees were soon permitted to return, the Jews were not allowed to go back until after the British conquest of Palestine in the summer of 1918. The deportation was committed by the Turks in compliance with the order of the same Ahmed Djemal who was one of the Young Turk triumvirate leaders. Some 10,000 Jewish deportees were evacuated from Tel Aviv. Many perished during the harsh winter of 1917– 18 – mostly from hunger and disease, though nowhere near on the same scale as that of the three Christian populations. Altogether, perhaps up to 1,500 Jews died as a result of Turkish measures (Segev 2009).

For decades, all charges of Ottoman genocide have been met with fierce resistance from successive Turkish governments. Those advocating it, or even mentioning the "g" word, have been prosecuted with lengthy jail terms. One of the most frequent counters made by the Turks and their supporters has been that what happened was actually a civil war, in which more Turks were killed than Armenians, having arisen as a result of Armenian deceitfulness in joining with the invading Russians in 1914. This idea of Armenians provoking the Turks has become known as the "provocation thesis," according to which the Armenians were viewed as a fifth column prepared to stab the Turks in the back as soon as the war situation allowed. The thesis was, however, a propaganda device fabricated in May 1915 by Turkey's German ally (Melson 1992: 10–12; Suny *et al.* 2011: 24–27).

Ever since then, the thesis has provided Turkish nationalists with a powerful weapon of persuasion to justify their denial that there ever was genocide. Arguments questioning the veracity of claims of a Turkish genocide of the Armenians, Greeks, and Assyrians during and after the First World War have existed for many decades, and have usually taken one of four basic forms: the destruction of the Armenians at the hands of the Turks never happened; that Turkey is not responsible for the vast number of Armenian deaths, which happened instead as a result of disease and starvation accompanying the deportation of Armenians out of war zones; that the term "genocide" is inapplicable owing to the fact that there was no intent on the part of the Young Turk government to destroy the Armenian population; and, finally, that any deaths that did occur were the result of a destructive civil war in the Ottoman Empire. These assertions, individually and collectively, have been made by successive Turkish governments and their supporters since the 1920s, and are still prevalent today. The most recent areas in which claims of an Armenian genocide have been contested are in academia (through the establishment of Turkish-funded chairs of Turkish Studies dedicated to a "no genocide" position), and in political campaigns lobbying legislatures against voting on propositions recognising the genocide (Akçam 2012: 373–447).

As denial of the genocide is Turkish state policy, it differs from most other forms of genocide denial which are, for the most part, conducted by individuals or organisations acting in a private capacity. For several decades, Turkish governments were in some ways successful in their worldwide advocacy of the "no genocide" position, but in recent years several states and international organisations have rejected Turkish denialism and passed resolutions acknowledging the genocide. Moreover, the European Union has made oblique references to Turkish accession being dependent upon a public recognition of the genocide's historical reality.

Turkish government denial as policy is not based on objective scholarship, but, rather, on political and racist foundations. Given this, the policy has often proceeded from the belief – often held with passionate conviction – that Turkey is struggling against a massive Armenian-centred conspiracy. As a result, the denialist stance has been maintained in spite of all evidence to the contrary.

There have been several challenges to the Turkish outlook, however. In April 2001, for example, New York Governor George Pataki (b. 1945) made an important statement in which he recognised the Armenian, Pontic, and Assyrian Genocides by name. In 2007, the International Association of Genocide Scholars resolved that the Ottoman campaign against the Christian minorities of the Empire constituted genocide. Most formally established university institutions dealing with Holocaust and genocide studies have recognised Ottoman actions towards the Empire's Christian populations between 1915 and 1923 as amounting to genocide. The governments of at least 21 countries, most states of the USA, and several states in other countries have recognised the veracity of the genocide and passed resolutions to that effect through their legislatures.

In order to give appropriate respect to the three genocidal experiences, it might be appropriate to refer to the Turkish campaign in broad terms, calling it genocide against the Christian population of the Ottoman Empire – the preference being to categorise all of the deaths and atrocities as being of a single cloth. There is, certainly, a remarkable similarity between them, even though all three peoples can refer to specific differences pertaining to each individual situation.

JUSTICE AND LEGACIES

On May 24, 1915, with accounts of the genocide being continually reported internationally, the forces opposed to Turkey – Britain,

France, and Russia – issued a formal warning to the Empire's leaders. In the first formal use of the term "**crimes against humanity**" in diplomatic discourse, this warning noted the nature of the offences being committed by the Young Turk regime, and warned that the guilty officials would be punished.

After the war, however, the Allies' attention was directed to other priorities. France focused its attention on punishing Germany; Russia was engulfed in revolution; and, despite the efforts of Ambassador Morgenthau, the United States did not take steps towards the punishment of the Young Turks. Only Britain showed any interest in pursuing post-genocide justice.

In 1919 the Sultan, under pressure from British occupation authorities, ordered domestic Turkish courts martial to try the Young Turk leaders, and by April of that year over 100 officials from the former regime were under arrest. Four major trials then began, and the first verdicts handed down found the defendants guilty of organising deportations, murder, pillage, robbery, and crimes against humanity and civilisation. However, international politics intruded into the process and undermined the domestic tribunals. As the British presence shrank, substantial numbers of accused Turks began being released.

Giving up on the prospect of any success through the domestic courts, the British decided to take custody of 68 of the most prominent prisoners accused of committing the most heinous crimes, and transferred them to a British detention centre in Malta for trial. Further problems ensued, however, when it was realised that the massacres, having been carried out under Ottoman law, were not the domain of British administration. International law against massive human rights abuses had yet to be developed, but in August 1920 the Treaty of Sèvres, the Allied **peace** treaty with Turkey, was signed; this included five articles on war crimes including language calling for Turks guilty of criminal acts to be brought before the military tribunals. The British, unsure of which way to turn, began to lose their nerve, and in August 1921 all Turks remaining in British custody were freed.

The genocide left a number of legacies. Those who survived were scattered in a global diaspora. All that remains today of historic Armenia is a small, landlocked state carved out of the former Soviet Union; there is practically no Greek community left in Turkey; and the Assyrians, devoid of a state of their own, struggle to have their historical experience as a distinct people acknowledged.

Moreover, the Ottoman genocides became an important precedent for later human rights violations. They drew attention to the dangers of international inactivity and failing to confront genocide denial. And, as will be shown later in this book, the consequences of allowing the perpetrators to go unpunished contributed to subsequent genocides.

DISCUSSION QUESTIONS

- Should the Armenian Genocide be recognised by the United Nations and individual countries within the international community?
- Can a government be justified in removing and destroying an entire population on the grounds of "military necessity"?
- Was the Armenian Genocide an example of the modern state and technology working together for destructive ends?
- In view of the fact that the Ottoman Turks also targeted the Assyrian and Greek populations of the Empire as well as Armenians, would it be more accurate to refer to a "Christian Genocide" as having taken place?

4

THE HOLOCAUST

A BRIEF OUTLINE

The Holocaust (in Hebrew, *Shoah*) is the term in English most closely identified with the attempt by Germany's National Socialist (Nazi) regime, together with its European allies, to exterminate the Jews of Europe during the Second World War. While an exact number of those murdered is impossible to determine, best estimates settle at a figure approximating around six million Jews, one million of whom were children under the age of 12, and 500,000 of whom were aged between 12 and 18 (Laqueur 2001: 115).

The intellectual, social, and theological roots of the Holocaust were very deep. Nazi anti-Semitism built on a much longer-lasting hatred of Jews as a people and the Jewish religious tradition, but with an important variation. The origins of anti-Jewish antipathy can be found in the Hebrew Bible (that is, the Old Testament), but the Christian New Testament's accusation that the Jews were responsible for the murder of Jesus saw religious and theological justifications for Jew-hatred. By the Middle Ages, the violence of religious anti-Semitism saw Crusades, pogroms, and persecutions, based on spurious accusations that Jews murdered innocent Christian children to drain their blood for the preparation of unleavened bread during Passover, and had poisoned wells resulting in the Black Death. While throughout much of European Christendom the Jews were demonised for their religion, this in itself does not explain the Holocaust. Conversion to Christianity, in most cases, spared converts from any further harassment.

Along with being forbidden from owning and farming land, however, the rise of mercantilism and capitalism in Europe left unconverted Jews, who could not join guilds, as economic (as well as religious) outsiders. The advancing secularisation of civil society accompanying the European Enlightenment brought new forms of social and political anti-Semitism to the fore.

The ultimate expression of anti-Semitism in the nineteenth century, which saw Jews constructed as a biological category and Jewish identity as innate, created the pre-conditions for the most violent expression of anti-Semitism – its racial manifestation as advocated by the Nazis.

National Socialism (Nazism) was a political movement founded in Germany. Intimately connected with the life and career of its leader, Adolf Hitler (1889–1945), it attained office on January 30, 1933 having been appointed by President Paul von Hindenburg (1847–1934).

To a large degree, Nazism began as a movement inspired by the growth of European **fascism**, but it incorporated a powerful and uncompromising strain of anti-Semitism – together with a racial conception of how the world operated – into its world view. Like fascism, its essential beliefs were grounded in a vigorous opposition to alternative ideologies, particularly Marxism, socialism, liberalism, and individualism. Hitler's philosophy called for an unyielding obedience of the people to the state, which was the transmitted will of the *Volk* (people). As leader (*Führer*) of the Nazi party, Hitler was the embodiment of the state and supreme arbiter of the *Volk*'s will.

The major goals of the Nazi state were physical expansion in accordance with the principle of racial unification; eradication of the nation's racial and political enemies; and the regimentation of society in every respect. Possessing radical ideas regarding society, the economy, and the nature of politics, German National Socialism was essentially destructive; through harnessing the power of an advanced industrial state to an ideology predicated on racial hierarchy, military power, expansion, and social engineering, it rapidly showed itself to be harmful, bellicose, and a model for all genocidal political movements.

Regarding the roots of the Holocaust, consideration must be given to the Versailles Peace Treaty of 1919, which ended the First World War. According to the terms of the treaty, Germany was to surrender significant parts of its national territory to surrounding states, as well as its entire overseas colonial empire; reduce its standing army to only 100,000 men; admit full responsibility and guilt for the Great War; and pay massive reparations, or compensation.

Hitler referred to Versailles as a *"Diktat"* ("dictated peace"), and used the document as one of the primary arguments for revenge against Jews, communists, socialists, and others who, he said, not only contributed to Germany's defeat in 1918, but were primarily responsible for the country's continuing social, political, economic, and military devastation during the years before his accession to office in 1933. Versailles, he asserted, was an instrument of world Jewry's attempt to reduce Germany to a vassal state. This, added to the general anti-Semitism that certainly preceded Hitler's ascent to office, provided an important outlet for his racial views of the world.

The granite foundation upon which his ideas rested saw the world in terms of superior and inferior human groups, of which the latter had only one function – to serve the former. The Jews were the exception: they had no place in the Nazi new order at all. Hitler saw that all human life constituted an ongoing confrontation for supremacy between competing races, a *Rassenkampf* ("racial struggle"). This struggle was both typified by and expressed at its most extreme through an abiding conflict between the Aryan "race" and the Jewish "race." The *Rassenkampf* was relentless, and had to be fought until the death of one of the two parties would see either an ideal future for the world under the unchallenged rule of the Aryans, or a hopeless future dominated by the forces of darkness unleashed by the "satanic Jew." The racial struggle, of necessity, had to be genocidal in scope; neither compromise nor mercy would ever be possible if the required victory was to be achieved. The only way to resolve the situation, therefore, was to arrange for the Jews' total disappearance from Germany. Different solutions were tried: voluntary emigration, forced emigration, and a variety of plans for deportation – to "the East," to Poland, to

Siberia, to the island of Madagascar. All these had to be dropped, however, with the outbreak of war in September 1939.

Furthermore, the suffering of the German people during the Depression, which led to massive hardship and poverty throughout much of society, permitted the transference of blame by the Nazis onto the Jews as a minority who were disproportionately represented in the professions, providing them with greater wealth and access to privilege.

The Nazis had already gained experience with systematic mass murder in the form of the so-called Euthanasia (or "T-4") Programme, whereby physically and psychologically disabled Germans were murdered by the state in the name of "selective breeding" for biological "purity." Later, during the Second World War, this quest would be translated into outright extermination.

The first step on the road to the Holocaust can be said to have taken place on the night of February 27, 1933, when Berlin's *Reichstag* (parliament building) was set on fire. The day after, on the pretext that the fire had been set by communists, Hitler persuaded President Hindenburg to sign a Decree for the Protection of the People and the State, suspending all civil and individual liberties. It empowered the government to take such steps as were necessary to ensure that the threat to German society was removed. In a mass crackdown, hundreds were detained in the first few days, and tens of thousands in succeeding weeks (Hett 2014).

Then, on March 20, 1933, *Reichsführer-SS* Heinrich Himmler (1900–45) announced the establishment of a prison compound for political detainees, about 15 kilometres north-west of Munich, on the outskirts of the town of Dachau. Many other camps, also intended as places of political imprisonment, soon followed. They removed opposition from the midst of the community, and intimidated the population into accepting the Nazi regime.

Jews were among those arrested for transgressing within the framework of the existing political classifications, but from 1935 onwards they were frequently being victimised for their Jewishness alone, due largely to the effects of the so-called Nuremberg Laws on Citizenship and Race. According to these laws, the formal status of Jews in the Nazi state was defined and put into practice. The Nazis defined Jews racially, with one Jewish grandparent sufficing to classify a person as Jewish. Henceforth, Jewish businesses were boycotted, Jewish doctors were excluded from public hospitals and only permitted to practice on other Jews, Jewish lawyers and judges were dismissed and disbarred, and Jewish students were expelled from universities. Jews were increasingly excluded from participation in all forms of German life. The Nuremberg Laws also withdrew German citizenship from Jews. It became illegal for a Jew and a non-Jew to marry or engage in sexual relationships. Life was to be made so intolerable that Jews would seek to emigrate; those who did not often found themselves arbitrarily arrested and sent to concentration camps. These arrests did not become widespread until 1938, and in most cases the victims were only held for a short time. The intention was to terrorise them into leaving the country.

The first large-scale arrests of Jews were made after November 9, 1938 as "reprisals" for the assassination in Paris of German consular official Ernst vom Rath (1909–38) by Jewish student Herschel Grynszpan (1921–40). The event precipitating these arrests has gone down in history as *Kristallnacht*, the "Night of Broken Glass." The resultant pogrom was portrayed by the Nazis as a righteous and spontaneous outpouring of anger by ordinary German people against all Jews, even though for the most part it was Nazis in plain clothes who whipped up most of the violence on the streets. This saw greater concentrated destruction than any previous anti-Jewish measure under the Nazis, and spelled out to those Jews who had, until now, thought the regime was a passing phenomenon that this was not the case (Schwab 1990).

Jews were now targeted for their Jewish identity alone. The November pogrom had the effect of transforming earlier legislative measures against Jews into physical harassment on a broader and more indiscriminate scale than ever before. From now on, overt anti-Semitic acts became state policy. As Germany's Jews began frantically seeking havens to which they could emigrate, however, the countries of the Free World began to close their doors. And, with Hitler's foreign policy appetite growing and new areas becoming annexed to the Third Reich, the number of Jews coming under Nazi control increased to less manageable proportions.

After Germany invaded Poland on September 1, 1939, a system of ghettos was established almost immediately in order to confine and concentrate Poland's Jewish population. Here, they were persecuted, terrorised, starved, and deprived of all medical care.

It can be said that the process of mass extermination really began only after Operation Barbarossa, the German invasion of the Soviet Union, on June 22, 1941. The invasion was accompanied by an order from Hitler in which he reinforced his often proclaimed role of saviour of Europe against Bolshevism. On June 6, 1941, prior to Barbarossa, Hitler issued his *Kommissarbefehl* ("Commissar Order") in which he directed that any Soviet cadres and political leaders captured would be summarily executed (Fritz 2011: 68–69). By extension, within the Nazi conception of **communism**, this included all Jews, as they were viewed as the chief disseminators of Bolshevik ideology.

Accordingly, in the weeks following Barbarossa, mobile killing squads known as *Einsatzgruppen* ("Special Action Groups") were established to follow the German combat troops. These squads were tasked with the total annihilation of all Jews in the newly conquered areas. Between 1941 and 1943, it is estimated that more than 1.4 million Jews were murdered (Bauer 1982: 200).

The initial means by which the *Einsatzgruppen* operated was to round up their captive Jewish populations – men, women, and children – take them outside village and town areas, force them to dig their own graves, and then murder them by shooting. When the repetition of that activity proved psychologically taxing, mobile gas vans using carbon monoxide were brought in, both to remove the intimacy of contact and to sanitise the process. While technologically at times quite inefficient, from an economic perspective it was a cost-effective use of both men and material.

It is not known precisely when the decision to exterminate the Jews of Europe was made, though best estimates settle on some time in the early summer of 1941. On January 20, 1942, a meeting of 15 high-ranking Nazis, representing the leading departments and agencies responsible for Jewish affairs in the Nazi empire, met at a villa in Wannsee, Berlin, to coordinate the actions required for the mass-murder campaign. The minutes of the meeting made it clear that the Nazis intended to extend their "final solution of the Jewish question" to Britain and all the neutral states in Europe, such as Ireland, Switzerland, Turkey, Sweden, Portugal, and Spain (Gilbert 1986: 280–285). In the months following, the Nazis enlarged or established a number of camps in Poland for the express purpose of killing large numbers of Jews. These camps – Auschwitz-Birkenau,

Bełzec, Chełmno, Majdanek, Sobibór, and Treblinka – were a departure from anything previously visualised, in both their design and character. With the exception only of Auschwitz, they did not perform any of the functions – political, industrial, agricultural, or penal – attributed to those further west or north. They were the *Vernichtungslager*, the death or extermination camps, institutions designed to methodically and efficiently murder millions of people in specially designed gas chambers, employing carbon monoxide from diesel engines (either in fixed installations or from mobile vans), or crystallised hydrogen cyanide which on contact with air oxidised to become hydrocyanic (or prussic) acid gas (Arad 1987; Longerich 2010).

As the Nazi armies on the Eastern Front began to retreat before the advancing Soviet forces (and later from American and British troops in the West), renewed efforts were made to annihilate the Jews while there was still time. Then, in March 1944, a shock of cataclysmic proportions fell upon the Jews of Hungary, the last great centre of Jewish population still untouched by the Holocaust. Over 500,000 Jews were murdered in the space of four months, with the killing facilities working non-stop, day and night. This was the fastest sustained killing operation of any of the Nazi campaigns against Jewish populations in occupied Europe (Braham 2000; Braham and Miller 1998; Vági *et al.* 2013).

When viewing this campaign in Hungary and the means employed to attain it, one reservation must be made: Bełzec, Treblinka, Sobibór, and Chełmno had by this time already been evacuated. Only Auschwitz remained to carry out the massive undertaking of spring 1944, as April had already seen the start of the evacuation of Majdanek. With the Soviet armies continuing their advance towards Germany throughout the latter half of 1944, the position of Auschwitz itself seemed uncertain. The earliest date of free contact with Soviet forces was January 22, 1945; when the site was formally occupied two days later, there were only 2,819 survivors left (Bartrop 2000: 19).

Most of the prisoners still alive in the eastern camps at the end of the war had by this time already been evacuated by the Nazis so as not to fall into the hands of the advancing Russians. The "death marches" that followed saw vast numbers of prisoners die while en route. Evacuated in the winter and early spring of 1944–45, they had to contend with bitter cold, fatigue, hunger, and the brutality of the SS guards, and for those who had already reached the limit of their endurance the death marches could have only one result. Often, the Russians were so close while the prisoners were marching away that the sounds of battle could be clearly distinguished, further adding to their distress. When they arrived at their new destination their trials were hardly eased, as they faced massive overcrowding in the camps to which they had been evacuated.

The prisoners were dumped into places like Bergen-Belsen to await liberation through death or an Allied victory. Painfully slowly, however, as German units everywhere surrendered, the camps were liberated. On April 12, 1945 the camp at Westerbork, in the Netherlands, was set free. The day before, Buchenwald's inmates rebelled against their SS guards and took over the camp, handing it to the Americans on April 13. Bergen-Belsen was liberated by the British Army on April 15, and on April 23 the SS transferred Mauthausen to the International Committee of the Red Cross. The next day, Dachau was overrun by the US Army. Five days later, on April 29, Ravensbrück was liberated. Theresienstadt was handed over to the Red Cross by the Nazis on May 2, and on May 8 American troops took control from the Red Cross of Mauthausen, the last major camp to be liberated in the West (Bridgman 1990; Abzug 1985).

THE VICTIMS

About two out of every three Jews living in Europe before the war were murdered in the Holocaust. All of Europe's Jews were targeted for destruction: the sick and healthy, the aged and young, the rich and poor, the religiously observant as well as converts to Christianity.

The destruction, however, was not spread evenly. Despite the Nazi ambition to wipe out all of Europe's Jews, most of those who survived lived in areas not occupied by Germany: Allied states such as Britain and the eastern areas of the Soviet Union, together with neutral states like Spain, Turkey, Portugal, Switzerland, and Sweden. Most of Denmark's Jews were rescued *en masse* through being smuggled to Sweden, while the Jews of Bulgaria were saved owing to a refusal on the part of the Bulgarian government to allow their deportation. Tens of thousands of Jews also survived in German-occupied Europe. Some survived in the forests, fighting the Nazis as partisans; others lived in hiding, or managed to hold on as prisoners in concentration camps until liberation.

Vast numbers of others, including Roma, German and Austrian homosexuals, political dissidents, Russian prisoners of war, and Germans with physical or mental disabilities, also lost their lives, though the fundamental difference between their fate and that of the Jews is that the latter were targeted on account of their very birth, a fact embedded into the core of Nazi ideology (Berenbaum 1992).

Once in train, the killing was at its most severe in Eastern Europe. About 4.5 million Jews were killed in the Polish-Soviet area. Hundreds of thousands of Jews from the Netherlands, France, Belgium, Czechoslovakia, Yugoslavia, and Greece were also murdered, for the most part deported to the Nazi killing centres in Poland. The Jews of Romania and Romanian-occupied territories were also slaughtered between 1941 and 1944. As mentioned previously, over half a million Hungarian Jews were murdered during the spring and summer of 1944 (Bauer 1982: 335).

Given this, it must be at all times remembered that the Holocaust was a deliberate and explicit attempt by the Nazis to destroy completely and permanently a Jewish presence in Europe. While all the others were also persecuted and in many cases murdered in huge numbers, it was the campaign against the Jews that was the ideological "ground zero" for Nazi racial ideology. Only the Jews were annihilated as part of a calculated policy of genocide.

An argument could be put that the Roma should also fall into this category. In late 1942, Himmler ordered that all Roma would be deported to Auschwitz-Birkenau, where they were set aside in a special "Gypsy camp" (*Zigeunerlager*). Most sent there did not live to see the liberation, killed by gassing or through disease, debility, or hard labour. Overall, the number of Sinti, Roma, and Lalleri whose lives were lost during the *Porrajmos* ("The Devouring") – that is, the whole period of the anti-Roma persecution by the Third Reich – is difficult to determine. So far as scholars can estimate, the number lies anywhere between a quarter and half a million, representing a percentage higher than that of most non-Jewish victims of the Nazis (Lewy 2000).

The fundamental difference between the experience of the Jews and the Roma is that, for the Nazis, the Jews formed a cosmic force that had to be destroyed for the good of all civilisation, whereas the Roma were victimised and murdered on the grounds of behaving in unsettled ways that did not fit ordered German social norms, of perceived inferior or mixed heredity, or of (as it was said) "innate criminality."

Despite a recent trend to include all those killed by the Nazis as victims of the Holocaust – thus leading some to refer, erroneously, to "11 million Holocaust victims" – the clearest definition of the Nazi terror lay in the deliberate attempt to annihilate every Jew who fell into the Nazi net. No other group was targeted in this way.

THE PERPETRATORS

Who were the perpetrators of these crimes? For the mother forced to choose between two children on the ramp at Auschwitz, it was the Nazi doctor forcing the choice. For the adolescent girl torn from the embrace of her little sister because she was old enough to work while the younger girl was not, it was an SS officer. For the old man beaten to death by the side of the road by a Nazi soldier because he couldn't move fast enough when ordered to, it was that soldier. And for the newlyweds who were forced into the squalor of the ghetto where the bride watched her husband die of starvation and disease, only to die herself immediately afterward, the Holocaust was represented by the soldiers who brought them into this condition.

Moreover, one did not have to be a German in order to be an oppressor. This was made clear through the experiences Jews had with the Arrow Cross party in Hungary, the Hlinka Guard in Slovakia, anti-Semitic Poles who denounced Jews to their German occupiers, Vichy French officials and police, Ukrainian collaborators, and so on. For many people who never saw a Nazi German, the Holocaust was visited upon them by a wide variety of messengers.

While an immediate response to the question of "who were the perpetrators of the Holocaust?" might settle on the person of Adolf Hitler, it must always be borne in mind that Hitler could not have achieved the destruction of the European Jews unaided. Within Nazi Germany, all sectors of society played their role in planning, facilitating, and executing what was euphemistically termed the "Final Solution." They ranged from the major leaders of the Nazi party – Hitler, Himmler, Hermann Göring, Josef Goebbels (1897–1945), Reinhard Heydrich (1904–42), and many others – through to bankers, senior officers of the German Army, police, civil servants, university academics, railwaymen, chemists, doctors, journalists, engineers, and the judiciary. Not all were necessarily aware of the full extent of the role they were playing, but all fitted into the bigger picture, and few questioned what the logical outcome of their actions could be.

Perhaps the most important agent of death was the SS (*Schutzstaffel*), an arm of the Nazi party that was formed in 1923 as a specialised unit of 50 men to act as Hitler's personal bodyguard. The SS was given its direction under the leadership of Himmler, who conceived of a paramilitary organisation consisting of members of high moral calibre, honesty, and decency, committed to the Nazi vision and agenda, and thoroughly anti-Semitic in orientation. Its infamous black uniform and *Totenkopf* (or "Death's Head") insignias were introduced in 1932. By 1933, it was a force of more than 200,000 men. Under Himmler's guidance, the SS not only developed the Nazi concentration camp system, but also took responsibility for staffing the camps, instituting the discipline policies within them, and planning how best to exploit the prisoners as slave labour. From the summer of 1941 onwards, the SS controlled the annihilation of Europe's Jews, first through the *Einsatzgruppen* and then, after 1942, through the extermination camps (Reitlinger 1956; Weale 2012).

Many Nazis of high rank (though not Hitler or Göring), as well as many members of the SS, were well educated. Goebbels held a PhD from the University of Heidelberg; Himmler studied agronomy at the Munich *Technische Hochschule* (now the University of Technology, Munich); Hans Frank (1900–46), appointed Governor-General of occupied Poland, was a lawyer, as were a majority of the 15 attendees at the Wannsee Conference in January 1942. Alfred Rosenberg (1893–1946), the Nazi party's leading race ideologue, possessed a PhD in engineering. Three out of the four commanders of the *Einsatzgruppen* operating in the Soviet Union had earned doctorates. The list goes on. These were all part of a genocidal project that formed a central platform of the Nazi state.

After the war, it was recognised that many people involved in the process of murder had volunteered eagerly for their task. Others, however, always saw themselves as simply obeying orders, such as several members of Reserve Police Battalion 101, a unit of 500 middle-aged, lower- and lower-middle class family men from Hamburg, who were drafted into the so-called "Order Police" and were active in murdering up to 38,000 men, women, and children in 1942 and 1943 (Browning 1992). A variety of hypotheses can be proffered regarding their behaviour: wartime brutalisation, racism, segmentation, and routinisation of their tasks, careerism, obedience to authority and orders, ideological indoctrination, conformity, quasi-military status, and a sense of elitism. Anti-Semitism must, of course, also be considered. No single explanation, however, provides an all-embracing explanation.

RESISTANCE, RESCUE, AND HELPING

Jews and non-Jews, as well as states and governments conquered or dominated by Nazi Germany, engaged in resistance activities throughout the Second World War. Often, their aims differed substantially. For non-Jews, the primary task was to overthrow the Nazi oppressors and restore their states to sovereignty. For Jews, in a world which permitted them few opportunities for escape or freedom, resistance efforts were primarily directed to survival in the first instance, followed by punishment of the enemy wherever possible – or, if all else failed, to face an inevitable death with dignity. Jews were frequently disadvantaged, however, because of the hostility of the surrounding populations and their reluctance to provide aid. In the ghettos and in the concentration and death camps, resistance, frequently in the form of sabotage (destruction of property, theft of goods, and the like) took place.

In some locations, particularly many of the ghettos of Poland, open and armed rebellion took place. Jews also participated in both partisan and underground movements throughout the war, though frequently they experienced localised forms of anti-Semitism at the hands of those opposed to the Nazis. All of these examples are testament to the fact that Jews did fight back, and that the post-war accusation that Jews went willingly to their deaths "like lambs to the slaughter" was, in fact, far from accurate (Tec 2013).

Some non-Jews also provided assistance, where they could. Individuals in every European country risked their lives to help Jews, even though rescuing was far from easy. Every day threw up complications in trying to secure a person in hiding, feed them, care for their medical needs, and the like. Still, thousands, for various reasons, provided help. This was a time when living space, food, sanitation facilities, and medicine were at a premium, and those who hid Jews risked their own lives as well as those of their families. Given the enormous perils involved in undertaking rescue efforts, it is remarkable that any of these initiatives took place at all. Depending on where one was located, people caught hiding Jews were, more often than not, executed immediately – either on the spot, or later, in public as an example to others.

With this in mind, one salient fact is worth remembering: that it was not easy being a rescuer. To stand out from the crowd, to refuse to acquiesce, to not compromise one's own values in order to guarantee personal safety at the expense of that of others – these were (and are) gruelling issues for people to confront when exposed to extreme situations.

By an Act of Israel's Knesset (parliament) in 1953, those who placed themselves at risk to aid and/or rescue Jews have been recognised as "Righteous among the Nations" (Hebrew, *Hasidei umot haolam*). Such acts included sheltering Jews seeking to avoid capture by the Nazis, supplying false documents, providing food, clothing, and shelter, and guiding Jews to places of safety, among many other rescue efforts. Those who are recognised as "Righteous" have been honoured at Yad Vashem, Israel's Holocaust memorial authority in Jerusalem (Gilbert 2002).

Several thousand have been acknowledged in this way, though some names stand out in public memory, even today. These include the Swedish diplomat Raoul Wallenberg (1912–47?), whose efforts saved up to 100,000 Jews in Hungary; the German businessman Oskar Schindler (1908–74), whose factory served as a refuge for over 1,200 Jews while still producing goods for the German war effort; the Swiss Vice-Consul to Budapest, Carl Lutz (1895–1975), who, similarly to Wallenberg, used his influence to guarantee the lives of over 62,000 Jews in Hungary; and an Italian citizen, Giorgio Perlasca (1910–92), who posed as a Spanish diplomat in order to save over 5,000 Jews in Budapest (Paldiel 1993; Paldiel 2000).

To these names should be added the pastor of the French village of Le Chambon-sur-Lignon, André Trocmé (1901–71) and his wife Magda (1901–96), who, providing a lead to the rest of the village, saved the lives of over 3,500 Jewish children (Hallie 1994). Other well-known examples of rescuing include the Japanese Vice-Consul in Lithuania, Chiune "Sempo" Sugihara (1900–86), who issued transit visas to thousands of Jewish refugees for travel to Japan (Levine 2012). In like manner, the Portuguese Consul in Bordeaux, France, Aristides de Sousa Mendes (1885–1954), provided transit visas to anyone who could present him with papers to stamp (Fralon 2001).

While some individuals worked to save the lives of Jews, only in two countries could it be seen that rescue was elevated to national policy – and even that was spontaneous, and, at first, the work of inspired individuals.

In Denmark, when the round-up and arrest of all of Denmark's 7,800 Jews was ordered for October 1, 1943, only a very few could be found. The whole community had been tipped off two days before by a German diplomat, Georg Ferdinand Duckwitz (1904–73). Phone calls were placed, homes were opened as safe houses, and arrangements were made to spirit Jews to the countryside. Then, wherever possible, a safe passage was arranged across the water to neutral Sweden. While some Jews were transported in large fishing boats, many others – individuals or small families – were ferried to freedom in much smaller vessels, even rowboats.

In what became a national underground project, both the organised Danish resistance movement and everyday citizens worked to evacuate as many members of the Jewish community as could be located. The action of the Danish people in rescuing their Jewish population is considered one of the most effective actions of collective resistance to Nazi repression (Lidegaard 2013; Goldberger 1987).

The actions of the government of Bulgaria in March 1943, like those of Denmark (but in an entirely different sense), are also worthy of note. Largely through the efforts of the Deputy Speaker of the Bulgarian parliament, Dimitar Peshev (1894–1973), Bulgaria managed to save its entire Jewish population of 48,000 from deportation after Germany demanded it do so. While this did not save the Jews from Bulgarian-occupied areas in Thrace and

Macedonia, no Jews were deported from Bulgaria proper (Bar-Zohar 1998; Chary 1972).

Those who rescued Jews during the Holocaust, regardless of how many they saved, demonstrated that there were ways out of this most awful of situations. It must always be remembered, however, that their actions, though outstanding examples of goodness in the face of genocidal evil, managed to save only a tiny proportion of those whose lives the Nazis already considered to be forfeited.

BYSTANDERS AND INTERNATIONAL REACTIONS

While many in occupied Europe agreed that Nazi actions against Jews were vicious, violent, inhumane, and morally wrong, it took exceptional courage and commitment to stand against them.

During the Holocaust, a bystander was one who was aware of the perpetration of Nazi crimes but did nothing to halt them. Individuals and organisations fell into this category for various reasons. Some, for example, were hostile towards the Jews, though not so much as to want to carry out harmful actions against them. As in any society, some were simply apathetic regarding what was happening to those around them. Others – often a majority – genuinely feared for their lives or those of their loved ones should there be repercussions for speaking out against the Nazi measures (and, even more so, for attempting to halt them). Further, the benefits that some people received through the dispossession and murder of the Jews added to the mix of why a person might stand by and not wish to get involved. There are, of course, many other reasons as to why bystanders did not speak out.

While the Holocaust did not introduce the phenomenon of the bystander, it nonetheless illustrated the consequences of indifference and passivity towards the persecution of others. One of the many factors militating against action was ignorance. Nazi actions, though coordinated throughout the Reich, were not conveyed to the peoples over whom the Nazis ruled, and besides, the Nazis had in any case effectively taken over all news outlets in Germany by the mid-1930s. Within Germany, people could only act on the information they had available to them – and no-one, outside of a very few at the highest levels of the government, had any idea of the big picture. Once war broke out in 1939, control over information became even tighter, and spread throughout all of occupied Europe. The Nazi regime used tactics of fear and terror to suppress any possibility of resistance or rescue, and for the most part (with a few important exceptions) any efforts to do so were only localised and not national in scale. All too often, moreover, there were no means to resist, and some bystanders were literally paralysed with fear or helplessness.

Individuals, groups, and entire nations were forced to make choices as to whether or not to resist the Nazis and rescue Jews (and other victims), and remaining silent often became a daily torment. The issues raised by such situations provoked profound moral and civic questions, though often people were under too much stress to consider them at the time: under what circumstances could injustice and Nazi violence be confronted? Further, knowing of this, was it possible to do anything so long as the injustice was sustained? As with all such moral questions, the answers were not easy of resolution, and had to be considered on a case-by-case, and individual-by-individual, basis.

So, too, was the role of the international community, which, being highly complex and detailed, cannot be summarised easily. Before 1939 the major international responses to the Nazi persecution of the Jews in Germany and Austria ranged between avowed horror and indifference. Rarely was any serious action taken against the Nazi regime, though in the early days several Nazis were concerned that internal anti-Semitic measures might have a negative impact on Germany's economy should other countries respond to defend the Jews' human rights. Such action, however, never materialised.

The major international response to Nazi measures against the Jews during the 1930s took the form of restrictive refugee immigration policies. Just as the Nazis were keen for Jews to leave Germany, most countries of the world sought to deny them entry. The Evian Conference, called by US President Franklin D. Roosevelt (1882–1945) in March 1938 and convened in July that year, saw delegates from 32 countries meet to consider the resettlement of Jewish refugees from Germany and Austria. By the end of the nine-day meeting, no resolution for the alleviation of Jewish distress was reached, affirming for Hitler the unwillingness of the Western democracies to extend themselves on behalf of the Jews.

Once the war broke out in September 1939, however, the Allies were keen to find ways to paint their Nazi enemy in the worst possible light, and they used the Jewish question as a means to do this. Still, they did not extend their own efforts to rescuing Jews. The preference was always to assert that the best way to help those persecuted in Europe was to win the war, and that no other distraction could be allowed to stand in the way of achieving that objective.

On December 17, 1942, by which time Nazi Germany had deported more than two million Jews to death camps (and up to a million more had been murdered by the *Einsatzgruppen*), a joint statement was made simultaneously in London, Washington, and Moscow condemning Nazi mass murder. First, the statement identified specifically that the crimes being described were targeting Jews – not Allied nationals or citizens, but, explicitly, Jews. Second, the Allies promised to punish those perpetrating the crimes identified. And third, they had no hesitation in employing the word "extermination" to describe what they had by that stage categorised (Breitman and Lichtman 2013).

Such condemnation, the most damning indictment issued against Nazi mass murder to date, was in fact to be the only multilateral denunciation of German actions regarding Jews throughout the duration of the Holocaust. Before this time and subsequently, no other inter-Allied **declaration** mentioned the Nazi extermination policy in this manner (Gilbert 1981).

Jewish hopes were buoyed by the announcement, however, and at another conference, convened by Britain and the United States and held in Bermuda on April 19, 1943, some anticipated that definite action on behalf of the Jews would follow. The supposed purpose of the conference was to discuss the Jewish plight, but, held at this remote site in order to control the flow of information by the news media, no official representatives of Jewish organisations were permitted to attend, and the agenda was severely curtailed. The particularity of Jewish suffering was masked by use of the term "political refugees." The conference placed more attention on prisoners of war than on refugees; the possibility of Palestine, then under British control, as a site for refugees was not discussed; there was no debate entered into regarding any direct negotiations between the Allies and Germany; and even discussions of sending food parcels to those already incarcerated in the concentration camps was curtailed. At its conclusion, on May 1, 1943, the Bermuda Conference was viewed as more of a public relations exercise than a serious attempt to address the issue.

On another level, an alternative approach to assisting Europe's Jews saw requests to bomb the rail lines leading to Auschwitz (and even the camp itself). These led nowhere (Gilbert 1981; Neufeld and Berenbaum 2000). Another attempt saw an offer made by the man known as the "Architect of the Final Solution," SS *Obersturmbannführer* Adolf Eichmann (1906–62), to "sell" the Jews of Hungary late in the war in what became known later as the "Blood for Goods" scheme. The Allies refused to enter into negotiations over this proposal. Only in 1944, under pressure both inside and outside his government, did President Roosevelt call into being the War Refugee Board which, ultimately, was responsible for the saving of 200,000 victims (chiefly in Hungary, through the efforts of Wallenberg and others) (Breitman and Lichtman 2013: 262–275).

While the record of Allied governments in saving Jews was on the whole poor, international bodies such as the Roman Catholic Church and the International Committee of the Red Cross were hardly better – though both organisations have worked hard since 1945 to rehabilitate their reputations.

At the Vatican, Pope Pius XII (Eugenio Pacelli, 1876–1958), who was intensely opposed to communism, theologically conservative, and a Germanophile, repeatedly refused to offer any public condemnation of the Nazi assault against the Jews. Some have argued that his public silence and failure to speak out, given his position as the acknowledged moral voice of the Western world's conscience, could possibly have intensified the tragedy (Zuccotti 2002; Cornwell 1999). His supporters, on the other hand, hold that the actions of the Vatican to give comfort and succour to Jews, much of it in secret, were all done with the Pope's knowledge and support (Dalin 2005).

The International Committee of the Red Cross (ICRC), on the other hand, which also had a huge role to play internationally as the world's premier humanitarian organisation, did not issue a public appeal on behalf of the Jews, claiming that its policies of neutrality, impartiality, and confidentiality had to be measured against whatever good it was capable of doing – and what the effect would be if it was denied access to prisons, detention centres, concentration camps, and the like during the war. The ICRC's ability to see to its fundamental tasks – monitoring of prisoner conditions, carrying messages between prisoners and their families, advocating more humane conditions, providing food and other "comforts" for prisoners, delivering emergency aid to victims of armed conflicts, among others – was put under immense strain during the Holocaust, when the ICRC's mandate did not extend to civilian prisoners. Many critics, however, have argued that the ICRC failed during the Holocaust to live up to its mandate of serving populations in danger (Favez 1999). In an official statement made on January 27, 2005, the ICRC stated that Auschwitz represented the greatest failure in its history.

Overall, one of the key questions coming from the Holocaust has to be whether or not Allied actions – beyond winning the war – could have prevented it or reduced the number of those murdered by the Nazis and those supporting them. While there is no easy answer to this in view of the fact that things did not work out that way, there can be little doubt that the silence and inaction of the world community, in the face of overwhelming evidence to the contrary, resulted in the avoidable loss of countless lives.

CONSEQUENCES

When considering the consequences of the Holocaust, we must first ponder the enormous loss of life caused by the Nazis. Owing to the industrialised and impersonal nature of their mass murders, it has proven difficult to provide a single, definitive figure of Jewish losses, though most estimates have settled at approximately six million of those who inhabited the countries and regions of what became German-occupied Europe.

Owing to the fact that the Nazis transported the majority of their victims from one place to another in order to murder them, the names of some localities will forever be associated with mass annihilation and human destruction. The six death camps established by the Nazis in Poland – Auschwitz-Birkenau, Treblinka, Sobibór, Bełzec, Chełmno, and Majdanek – became the sites of the most horrific, purposeful, and sustained killing in the twentieth century.

The loss of two-thirds of European Jewry – representing more than one-third of the entire world's Jews in 1939 – led to devastating results from which the global Jewish population has not yet recovered. In 1939, there were 17 million Jews in the world, and by 1945 only 11 million. The loss of so many lives deprived the world of generations unborn, talent that did not see realisation, and contributions to civilisation that were never made. Most of the survivors, particularly in Eastern European countries, found they did not have homes to which they could return. Not only had their countries been devastated by the war, but in many cases they were not welcomed back into their original communities.

As a result, the Holocaust continued to torment the European Jewish community long after the killing stopped, as it ended communal life that in some cases stretched back beyond a thousand years. The war left hundreds of thousands of displaced Jews languishing in camps without a home. While a new dispersal out of Europe took place, the Holocaust also served to hasten the immigration of Jewish refugees to the Jews' ancestral homeland in Palestine, which in 1948 became the independent Jewish state of Israel. The distribution of the world's Jewish population now is completely different from what it was before the Second World War. Europe, where the Jewish presence was thoroughly devastated, gave way to Israel and the United States as Jewry's new population centres.

Beyond the killing, the Holocaust had other consequences. Prior to the Holocaust, the Nazi belief in eugenics – the science (some say pseudo-science) aimed at improving the genetic composition of a population – was a given within racial conceptions of the world. "Race hygiene" was understood to mean the improvement of the human species through selective breeding and the elimination of those hereditary factors that "weakened" the species. By the time the Nazis assumed power in 1933, they were able to apply such ideas to so-called "racial" categories, specifically Jews and Roma. Nazi scientists and propagandists were thereafter able to "prove" the inferiority of non-Aryan peoples, and thus lay the groundwork for the latter's ultimate extermination.

After the Holocaust, notions of eugenics and racial superiority were completely discredited. Ideas of racial anti-Semitism were exposed as fallacious, and the thought that a "superior" race could be bred artificially came to an ignominious end (other than in the view of those who refused to see the political dimensions of where their thinking could lead, namely to the Nazis' agenda of annihilation).

Another important consequence of the Holocaust came owing to the very scale of the destruction itself. After six years of total war and its accompanying massive loss of life, the Holocaust awakened the conscience of humanity. In 1945 there seemed to be no difficulty in people identifying the horror for what it was. People knew instinctively what the carnage represented for the future of the world, and reports through both official channels and the media had already been conveying for some time the realities of the Nazi Holocaust as evidence of one of the worst expressions of inhumanity. From this, the cry of "Never Again" was raised, resulting in two important initiatives: the quest for post-Holocaust justice, and a search for ways to ensure that it could never recur.

DISCUSSION QUESTIONS

- To what extent do you think the Holocaust can be described as "unique"?
- Did the countries of the Free World fail to rescue Jews during the Holocaust?
- Did Hitler and the Nazis plan the annihilation of the Jews from the very beginning of the Third Reich, or was the "Final Solution" something that evolved gradually over time?
- What were the means employed in order to achieve the "Final Solution"?
- Was the Holocaust a tragedy for the Jews, for the Germans, or for both? Why?
- Could any elements of the Holocaust have been foreseen in Nazi legislation before 1941?

5

GENOCIDE, ASIA, AND THE COLD WAR

THE NATURE OF THE COLD WAR

After the Second World War a state of extreme tension arose between the United States and the Soviet Union, who had divided into two armed camps based on irreconcilable ideological and political differences. The United States and its allies, the so-called "Western Bloc," were on one side, and the Soviet Union and its allies, the "Eastern Bloc," were on the other. Adhering to mutually incompatible political and economic beliefs and policies (the United States **democracy** and capitalism, the Soviet Union **totalitarianism** and socialism), they were embroiled in intense rivalry between 1945 and 1990. Both became major nuclear powers, and as they developed ever-more sophisticated weapons of mass destruction, tension between the two blocs heightened the possibility of nuclear war. Simultaneously, they engaged in fierce competition to sway other states to their policies, particularly in the Third World – where their support led to a number of brutal and bloody proxy wars. The conflict was fuelled by mutual distrust and suspicion, coupled with aggressive intelligence-gathering activities and the race for space and technological supremacy.

The term "Cold War" was first employed by US presidential adviser Bernard Baruch (1870–1965) in 1947, who contrasted this form of international tension with the "heat" of a shooting war (Baruch 1960: 388). Many of the features of modern warfare were present, such as an arms race, ideological divisions, propaganda, and espionage, but large-scale direct military confrontation or combat did not take place. Periodically, tensions heated up, though they never escalated into full-scale armed conflict.

As well as being the defining conflict of the second half of the twentieth century, the Cold War could also be intensely personal. Most clearly, in the early days of the confrontation US Presidents Harry S. Truman (1884–1972), Dwight D. Eisenhower (1890–1969), and John F. Kennedy (1917–63) saw themselves as engaged in a global struggle for supremacy with Soviet leaders Josef Stalin (1878–1953), Nikita Khrushchev (1894–1971), and Leonid Brezhnev (1907–82). Later, an "East–West thaw" began to surface under the initiatives of new Soviet rulers such as Mikhail Gorbachev (b. 1931) and Boris Yeltsin (1931–2007), and US President Ronald Reagan (1911–2004). In the Soviet Union, a new openness (Russian, *Glasnost*) was introduced alongside of the development of capitalism, and the stranglehold of the Communist Party over people's lives began to weaken. Ultimately, these forces, when combined, led to the collapse of the Soviet Union between 1989 and 1991.

The nature of the Cold War meant that the two superpowers frequently confronted each other through the votes they cast in the United Nations Security Council. This often resulted in stalemate situations when it came to taking action regarding genocide.

This was a period in which the world was confronted by an enormous number of stresses and strains: economic boom and bust, decolonisation and wars of liberation, social protest and wide-sweeping calls for change, and the biggest threat of them all: mutually assured total nuclear destruction. Those who had hoped to reduce or prevent genocide found that the powers had other issues with which to contend. In turning a blind eye here and there for the purpose of accommodating potential or genuine allies, dictatorial or authoritarian rulers were often able literally to get away with murder.

The second half of the twentieth century, as a result, began to appear as nothing other than a continual period of massacres and genocidal killing. Most of this was played out in Asia, where conflicts in Bangladesh, Cambodia, East Timor, and elsewhere stand out as models of what the world became during the Cold War. It was a time that had a devastating effect on post-1945 hopes that a new, non-genocidal system could be created throughout the world.

INDONESIA

On August 17, 1945, Indonesian nationalist leaders Sukarno (1901–70) – like most traditional Javanese, he was only given one name at birth – and Mohammed Hatta (1902–80) declared Indonesian independence from the Dutch colonisers who had been ruling the archipelago since the sixteenth century. As Dutch forces attempted to re-establish colonial rule, a vicious war erupted, resulting in victory for the rebels and complete independence by 1949 under Sukarno.

His pluralistic administration permitted a multi-party system that included the country's very large Communist Party of Indonesia (PKI), which grew to some two million strong by the mid-1960s. Within the Cold War context, this was seen as politically very dangerous by elements in the army, including a leading general, Suharto (1921–2008). Sukarno's approach permitted the PKI to gain influence in many sectors of society. By late 1965, the army was divided between a left-wing faction allied with the PKI, and a right-wing faction that was being courted by the United States (Mortimer 2007).

In this increasingly explosive situation, and in order to forestall the prospect of a possible communist takeover, any spark might be sufficient to cause the country to fall into a state of crisis. On October 1, 1965, it happened. Six senior Indonesian generals were kidnapped and murdered by junior officers; the PKI was blamed, and the military portrayed the murders as an attempted *coup d'état*. Suharto led a successful counter-*coup*, resulting in widespread reprisals against the communists – even though the role of the PKI was unclear. On October 16, 1965, under immense pressure from the army, Sukarno appointed Suharto as Minister for the Army and army commander-in-chief, after which Suharto ordered his forces to destroy the PKI and the threat it allegedly represented.

In the months that followed, the army led an anti-communist purge that saw an unprecedented explosion of violence sweep the country. PKI members (many of whom were, coincidentally, ethnically Chinese) were rounded up, tortured, and executed. Families of suspected communists were targeted by the army, by military endorsed militias, and even by civilian mobs. The number estimated killed varies widely; most accounts put the figure at about half a million, though two million has been speculated (Cribb 1990). Hundreds of thousands more were imprisoned without trial, often for periods of 20 years or longer. Under Suharto, the military forces were purged of what were viewed as pro-Sukarno elements, and Sukarno's power base effectively collapsed. On March 11, 1966, Suharto assumed supreme authority, displaced Sukarno, and introduced what became known soon afterwards as the New Order (*Orde Baru*). The next day, the PKI was officially banned, PKI members of parliament were purged, the press was gagged, and trade unions were forbidden. Suharto was appointed Acting President in 1967 and President the following year. He was to remain in office until he retired in 1998.

The upshot was that Indonesia would be ruled as an authoritarian quasi-democracy, increasingly bureaucratised and militarised, until Suharto left office. The military received a permanent place in running the country. The electoral system was modified to allow only "safe" political parties to run for office, and as a result Suharto was elected unopposed as President in 1973, 1978, 1983, 1988, 1993, and 1998. Speculation has been rife that Suharto's rule possibly saved Indonesia from going communist, but, by doing so, the Indonesian people suffered over 30 years of repression, censorship, and state-sanctioned violence.

BANGLADESH

The year 1965 saw skirmishes break out in April along the Pakistani–Indian border. These clashes spread to Kashmir, and developed into what became known as the Second Indo–Pakistani War. A ceasefire was arranged through the UN Security Council on September 23, 1965, and in the years that followed a very uneasy peace settled over the region.

In 1969, after a period of discontent prompted by corruption, a weak economy, and the casting of blame for Pakistan's defeat in the 1965 war, riots broke out across the nation as popular resentment boiled over against Pakistan's President, Ayub Khan (1907–74). On

March 25, 1969 he announced his resignation and handed the government over to the unrelated Brigadier-General Yahya Khan (1917–80), who immediately imposed martial law. The constitution was suspended, and the National Assembly dissolved. Pakistan, created by the British colonisers in 1947, was divided into two wings to the east and west of India. About the only thing they had in common was their majority Muslim religious identity: ethnically and linguistically, they were otherwise quite different from each other.

At the end of March 1970, Yahya introduced a new interim constitution, but this was overshadowed that August when disastrous floods devastated low-lying East Pakistan. The disaster gave impetus to the Awami League, a distinctly Bengali party (that is, from the Bay of Bengal, or East Pakistan) led by Sheikh Mujibur Rahman (1920–75). Citing the inadequacy of the response from West Pakistan, the League demanded regional autonomy for East Pakistan and an end to military rule. Yahya, in turn, organised the country's first nationwide direct elections on December 7, 1970, which took place with an unexpected outcome: the Awami League won 160 of the 162 seats allotted to the East, becoming the majority party in Pakistan's 313-seat National Assembly. Mujibur claimed government, and put forth a six-point programme for the future of Pakistan to be used as the basis of a new constitution (Jahan 2013).

On February 22, 1971, West Pakistan's military leaders decided not to back the new government, and to crush the Awami League which they saw as a direct threat to the country's unity. Politicians led by Zulfikar Ali Bhutto (1928–79) then pressured Yahya to cancel the inaugural sitting of the new National Assembly. Others saw this as an opportunity to do away once and for all with troublesome Bengali separatism (Bass 2013).

It is not exactly clear what Yahya's position was regarding the future. Some have claimed that he had a genocidal aim in mind to bring East Pakistan to heel. One oft-quoted comment attributed to him was that the state should kill three million Bengalis in order to ensure that the rest would toe the line. Whether or not he actually said this, the events that were subsequently played out, on his watch, indicate at least that he had little interest in their protection (Bartrop 2012: 335–338).

On March 25, 1971, an emergency plan developed by General Tikka Khan (1915–2002) went into operation. Roadblocks and barriers appeared all over East Pakistan's capital, Dhaka. The university was attacked, and students were murdered in their hundreds. Death squads roamed the streets, killing some 7,000 people in a single night (Bartrop 2012: 337).

The destructive tempo during these first days soon accelerated into a full-blown and brutal civil war. Within a week, half the population of Dhaka and the port of Chittagong had fled, and tens of thousands had been killed (Jahan 2013: 253). East Pakistanis saw little solution but to secede from the rest of the country, a move that was resisted from West Pakistan with staggering violence. Destroying the Awami League's ascendancy now became a crusade not only to terrorise East Pakistanis into accepting their *de facto* colonial status, but, as a bonus, to also rid the East of its large Hindu minority. No accurate estimate can be made of the number of people killed or wounded, or of women raped, but the assessment of international human rights organisations is that the crackdown may have resulted in the murder of up to three million people, and 200,000 women and girls raped. Ten million refugees fled to India, and 30 million were internally displaced (Jahan 2013: 250). A conclusion can be drawn that a calculated policy of genocide initiated by the government of West Pakistan was unleashed on the people of East Pakistan for what seemed to be the singular purpose of coercing them into accepting a continuance of Pakistani rule.

Yahya's onslaught led to a struggle for the liberation of what was now called Bangladesh, and eventually it drew India into a war with Pakistan to arrest the massive flood of refugees fleeing the mayhem in East Pakistan. On December 16, 1971, West Pakistani forces deployed in the East surrendered unconditionally to the Indians, and a day later Indian Prime Minister Indira Gandhi (1917–84) proclaimed a unilateral ceasefire.

Yahya resigned as Pakistani leader on December 20, 1971, and Bhutto became President. He revoked martial law, and purged the military of many of the officers who were seen to have lost the war. Pakistani prisoners of war were repatriated from India, though none were ever tried for war crimes. On February 22, 1974, Pakistan recognised Bangladesh, and on September 17 the same year

Bangladesh was admitted to the UN. Formal relations between Pakistan and Bangladesh were only established in 1976.

CAMBODIA

Four years after the nations of the world stood by while the Indian subcontinent erupted, communist leader Pol Pot (1928–98) and his Khmer Rouge comrades won a bloody civil war in Cambodia, and began one of the most radical attempts at remodelling an existing society the world had ever seen. In taking the Cambodian people back to the "Year Zero" (as Pol Pot put it), up to 1.7 million people lost their lives (Kiernan 2007: 549). The genocide happened between April, 1975 and January, 1979.

Pol Pot, born Saloth Sar to a well-to-do family in Kompong Thum province, was educated in the French colonial system, and qualified for a scholarship that led to advanced study in Paris. While in France between 1949 and 1953, he developed into a Cambodian (or "Kampuchean") nationalist, and gravitated towards the one movement that could offer a broad appeal to the mass of the working people: the Communist Party. In 1951, he joined a cell for Cambodians within the French communist party, the *Cercle Marxiste*. From this base, and after a great deal of underground activity, he and his Khmer Rouge supporters ("Red Khmers" or Cambodians) took control of the communist movement in Cambodia in 1966 (Short 2006).

The rise to power of the Communist Party of Kampuchea (CPK) must be fixed squarely within the Cold War environment of the 1960s and 1970s, and particularly the Vietnam War (1962–75). Taking advantage of the weakness of the US-backed government of Cambodian General Lon Nol (1913–85) and the political vacillation of King Norodom Sihanouk (1922–2012), Pol Pot and the Khmer Rouge waged an effective guerrilla war that saw the communists' assumption of power on April 17, 1975 (Kiernan 2004).

Pol Pot and the CPK immediately set about creating their new, "perfect," society. The Khmer Rouge carried out a policy that aimed to totally erase all signs of French colonial rule, and restore Cambodia to the presumed pristine condition prevailing before the foreigners had stamped their cultural traits on the land and its people. For nearly four years, Cambodia was brutally eradicated of any evidence of alien ways. The primary targets were the cities, in particular the capital, Phnom Penh. The city's population of nearly two million was uprooted and "resettled" in the countryside, so as to purge them of their exposure to what were deemed to be bourgeois ways. This would indoctrinate them, in turn, to rural, traditional Khmer culture, ostensibly unspoiled by colonialism and capitalism − the twin enemies of the anti-colonialist, communist, and mono-ethnic nationalist Khmer Rouge. Millions were forced to undergo "re-education," including public confessions in the course of which hundreds of thousands perished from exposure and lethal violence (Kiernan 2008).

The Khmer Rouge's fanaticism led to executions of "enemies" that covered the full spectrum of society. Intellectuals, artists, professionals, those who had travelled abroad, those who spoke a foreign language − in short, all who embodied "foreign" (that is, anti-communist or non-Khmer) ideals were systematically killed as having been too "contaminated" to participate in building the new society. In fact, the Khmer Rouge was so committed to destroying the old society and creating a new one that it eradicated even that most fundamental of social forms, the family; and this is to say nothing of such expressions of modernity as transportation, education, finance (including money), technology, administration, or governance. Henceforth, the national project would be dedicated to serving Angka, the "Organisation," from which all was to emanate in the new Democratic Republic of Kampuchea.

When the carnage was over, stopped by an invasion from Vietnam in January, 1979, it is estimated that at least one in four Cambodians had been killed. Among the dead, and targeted for extinction, were the country's minorities, including the Muslim Cham, ethnic Chinese and Vietnamese, and Buddhist monks. With the Vietnamese invasion, the Pol Pot government fell and the Khmer Rouge fled into the jungles of western Cambodia.

The response of the United States to the Cambodian genocide must be seen within the context of the Vietnam War. In the latter years of that conflict, the US had to cope with North Vietnamese supplies being sent to the Viet Cong via Cambodia. The United States' response to this was one of heavy bombing of the jungle trails used to smuggle these supplies, in order to disrupt the flow of

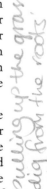

men and *matériel* through what was, in reality, neutral territory. This, in turn, strengthened the radical elements of the Khmer Rouge. With the end of the war in Vietnam, the administration of President Gerald Ford (1913–2007) was not inclined to get involved in the crisis in Cambodia. The public was deeply divided, and too emotionally exhausted to consider undertaking another foreign venture in Asia. In 1976, new President Jimmy Carter (b. 1924) endorsed this position. By 1979, when Pol Pot's regime was overthrown by Vietnam, the United States had done nothing to stem the tide of genocide in Cambodia, in large measure due to the prevailing domestic climate that rejected **intervention** as an option (Shawcross 1979).

The United States was not alone in its stance: allies such as Britain, Canada, France, and Australia essentially looked the other way as the Khmer Rouge attempted to restructure Cambodian society and, in doing so, committed genocide. In the Cold War environment, the Khmer Rouge was seen as the enemy of Vietnam, and, in a bizarre strategic game of prioritising, the countries of the West preferred to consider the communist Khmer Rouge as less of a threat than the communist Vietnamese.

EAST TIMOR

East Timor is an island nation situated between Indonesia and Australia. In 1702 it was formally declared a Portuguese colony (even though a Portuguese presence there had dated back to 1515), while the western half of the island was part of the much larger Dutch East Indies in what would later become Indonesia.

In 1974 a *coup* took place in Portugal, leading to that country's sudden withdrawal from its overseas empire. East Timor's colonial Governor, Mário Lemos Pires (1930–2009), announced immediate plans to grant the colony independence, even though next to nothing had been done to prepare the territory for decolonisation. In short time, however, a number of hastily formed political parties surfaced. Among these was a local Marxist group, the *Frente Revolucionária do Timor-Leste Independente* (Revolutionary Front for East Timor's Independence, or FRETILIN), founded on May 20, 1974.

FRETILIN was established for the purpose of securing independence. It had a strong radical socialist foundation, sought immediate independence, and claimed to speak on behalf of all East Timorese people. By December 1974, it had developed nationwide pro-grammes in education, social welfare, health, agriculture, literacy, and the like. FRETILIN ran into opposition from a rival party, the UDT (*União Democratica Timorense*, the Timorese Democratic Union), which was less radical and called for a more progressive and multi-stage timeline for independence that would be slanted towards some sort of federal model with Portugal. On August 11, 1975, the UDT staged a *coup*; for three weeks, civil war raged throughout East Timor as forces of the UDT battled with a hastily formed armed wing of FRETILIN, called FALINTIL (*Forças Armadas de Libertação Nacional de Timor-Leste*, National Liberation Forces of an Independent East Timor). Somewhere between 1,500 and 2,000 people died at this time (Dunn 2013: 295–296).

As FRETILIN became more influential, Cold War politics began to intervene. East Timor's huge neighbour, Indonesia, which had for a long time coveted the territory, began expressing concern that a socialist party should attain power so close to home. By September 1975, with FRETILIN's victory, Indonesia's policy on East Timor had hardened into direct opposition.

As the Portuguese administrators began to leave, FALINTIL troops seized the bulk of the colonial armoury, and, on November 28, 1975, the Democratic Republic of East Timor was proclaimed. Nine days later, on December 7, 1975, Indonesian military forces responded by invading.

In the first few days of the invasion, thousands of citizens of the capital, Dili, were killed, and a systematic campaign of human rights abuses commenced (Dunn 2013: 287). It was clear from the outset that this had the singular intention of intimidating the population and crushing the prospect of any resistance before it could get organised. What the Indonesians did not figure on, however, was the extent of difference between the two peoples. The East Timorese had (and have) a different ethnic identity to the Indonesians, spoke Tetum or Portuguese rather than Bahasa Indonesia, were almost exclusively Roman Catholic rather than Muslim, and had historically never been interested in aligning with Indonesia. As the Indonesians saw it, therefore, the only way they could absorb the territory as Indonesia's 27th state was through terror and military occupation.

The result was a series of campaigns resulting in mass murder, starvation, and death by torture. Within two months of the invasion, tens of thousands had been killed. Over the next three years, up to 200,000 people – that is, one-third of East Timor's inhabitants – had lost their lives (Charny 1999: 191; Shelton 2004: 273).

A large measure of the destruction was brought about through the government's policy of "Indonesianising" East Timor. This aimed to transform the personality of the territory from being a Portuguese colony with aspirations to independence, into being a fully fledged (and loyal) state of Indonesia. This was to be achieved in several ways: through the complete disruption (and then elimination) of regular East Timorese life and its replacement with a Javanese lifestyle; through the forcible removal of the population from large rural areas, and their relocation to newly created "strategic hamlets" (which some would later equate with *de facto* internment camps); and through the impact of these hamlets in the breaking up of traditional agriculture, trade, and village and family life. The overall impact of these measures saw food shortages and diseases, and the creation of a culture of dependence in which the population was forced to rely on Indonesian handouts for health services and medicine.

Indonesianisation also involved the repression of East Timorese culture, such that only Indonesian songs, dances, and the like were permitted publicly, while in education a purely Indonesian education system was introduced. Many new schools were established, but the curriculum was Indonesian, the language of instruction was Bahasa Indonesia, history lessons focused on Indonesian history only, and the study of East Timorese language or culture was forbidden.

Finally, the Indonesian authorities imposed a harsh regime of physical repression, by which all attempts from the East Timorese people to encourage or express their own culture were physically suppressed. People were often arrested and tortured, killed on the spot, or simply "disappeared." *Kopassus*, the Special Forces unit of the Indonesian Army, was given responsibility for ensuring that East Timorese resistance was minimised, and it did so through conducting what was effectively a terror campaign (Robinson 2010).

Initially, the Indonesian Army felt that it could crush FALINTIL easily and quickly, but soon found it was fighting a difficult war in harsh terrain. The consequence was a significant increase in combat forces. By late December, 1975, Indonesia had poured in a vast number of troops, who often behaved abominably. In September, 1977 the occupiers began interning civilians in an attempt to force a decisive confrontation with FALINTIL.

The main agent of repression was a military unit known as *Kolakops* (*Komando Pelaksanaan Operasi*, or Operations Implementation Command). Essentially responsible for counter-insurgency activities, the fact that *Kolakops* units were specially created and sat outside regular military command structures gave them wide discretionary powers not normally found in the Indonesian military's rules of engagement. Consequently, abuses of civilians, torture of prisoners, and localised massacres took place under *Kolakops* administration with **impunity**.

The best-known example of this took place on November 12, 1991, when mourners at the Santa Cruz cemetery in Dili were fired upon by *Kopassus* troops under *Kolakops* command, with substantial loss of life. The catalyst for the massacre was a funeral procession for an East Timorese student, Sebastião Gomes (1969–91), who had been shot dead by Indonesian troops a few days earlier. Tensions were already at flashpoint by the time of the funeral. A parliamentary delegation from Portugal had been due to arrive in East Timor to investigate allegations of human rights abuses, but, when student groups supporting FRETILIN threatened to turn the group's arrival into a protest demonstration, the authorities grew wary and stepped up the military presence throughout Dili. As the funeral procession approached the cemetery, some of the students took the opportunity to unfurl banners calling for independence. In the incendiary environment, this was the final justification the *Kopassus* forces needed to clamp down on the procession. When the march entered the cemetery, truckloads of troops appeared; shortly thereafter, they opened fire.

While figures regarding the numbers of killed and wounded in the ensuing violence vary, the most commonly accepted numbers are 271 killed, with hundreds more wounded and missing (Robinson 2010: 7; Dunn 2013: 291). The massacre was witnessed and filmed by Western journalists, and, after being smuggled out of East Timor, broadcast around the world to universal condemnation. The fact that *Kopassus* forces were at the cemetery on the day of the funeral, were heavily armed, and did not hesitate to open fire, indicated the likelihood that the action had been prepared in advance. The massacre at the Santa Cruz cemetery was a clear statement of the Indonesian government's determination to continue its repression of East Timor, and to maintain its ruthless control over the territory.

Over the two decades and more of Indonesian rule, the international response to all this was largely one of indifference. Indonesia's neighbour, Australia, was especially keen not to antagonise the populous nation to its north, and was the only country to recognise the *de jure* incorporation of East Timor into Indonesia, and to advocate Indonesia's case at the United Nations. There is substantial evidence that the United States endorsed the Indonesian takeover, and continued supplying weapons to assist the Indonesian military throughout the years of the occupation (Nevins 2005).

For its part, even though the United Nations passed numerous resolutions calling on Indonesia to withdraw, these were either ignored by the government in Jakarta, or not pushed hard enough by the Security Council. Within the Cold War context there was never a possibility that Suharto would align with the Soviet Union or China in the face of Western opposition, but the United States, anxious lest a hardline approach toward the occupation be seen by the Indonesians as a reason to look elsewhere for friends with which to side – for example, to the non-aligned nations – trod very softly on the whole issue, at least in public.

AFGHANISTAN

In April, 1978, a communist government under the People's Democratic Party of Afghanistan (PDPA) seized power in the capital, Kabul, and immediately set about the task of remodelling society. During the first 18 months of the regime, the intelligentsia was wiped out in the tens of thousands, and scores of thousands more fled to countries in the West. Opponents rebelled against the PDPA regime, in what quickly developed into a civil war. The government of neighbouring Pakistan provided the rebels with support, while the Soviet Union sent thousands of military advisers to support the PDPA (Bradsher 1999).

As Afghanistan was sliding towards chaos, Soviet troops invaded in December, 1979 in order to buttress the regime and install politicians who would maintain their fidelity towards the Soviet Union and communism.

Once the occupation of the country was an established fact, the Soviets were faced with constant guerrilla war from armed Afghan opponents calling themselves *mujahaddin* (fundamentalist Islamic freedom fighters). The Soviet strategy to combat their effectiveness took two forms. In the first, Soviet troops launched a systematic operation to depopulate certain regions so that the *mujahaddin* would be deprived of bases from which to launch their attacks; second, they initiated a military campaign in which modern firepower would shatter the ability of the insurgents to fight back. It was intended through this that so much destruction would take place that the civilian population would be deprived of the will to continue sheltering the *mujahaddin*. As military strategies these were effective over large parts of the country, but the toll on the Afghan people was catastrophic.

The major Cold War response to the invasion and occupation of Afghanistan came from the United States. Support for the *mujahaddin* came from the Reagan administration in the form of increased arms and funding, as the *mujahaddin* were clearly an anti-communist force waging a war of liberation against the communist (and, as it was seen, expansionist) Soviet Union.

It has been estimated that the military conflict claimed 180,000 Afghan casualties overall, with 90,000 killed. But civilian deaths numbered more than 1.5 million, representing 10 per cent of the total population (and 13.5 per cent of the male population). Some six million refugees fled to surrounding countries (Totten and Bartrop 2008: 4). Afghanistan was laid waste, with agricultural production and livestock numbers halved. The Soviet strategy of "rubblisation" returned the country to the Dark Ages, paving the way for a radicalisation of the survivors that would be realised in the decade after the Soviet departure in 1988.

KURDISTAN

The Kurds are the largest national entity in the world without a sovereign state of their own. Comprising anywhere between 25,000,000 and 35,000,000 people living primarily in four nation states – Iran, Iraq, Syria, and Turkey – they are a Muslim people who do not see themselves as Arabs and are united by language, culture, and history (Bartrop 2014).

Iraqi dictator Saddam Hussein (1937–2006) possessed what can only be described as an outright hatred of the Kurds, and was single-minded in his pursuit of their destruction. His cousin, Ali Hassan al-Majid (1941–2010), commonly known as "Chemical Ali," was Minister of Defence in Saddam's Ba'ath Party regime. He was known to be one of Saddam's senior advisers, and a brutally tough "enforcer" for the regime.

In March 1987, al-Majid was given the post of Secretary-General of the administrative zone called the Northern Bureau, the location of Iraqi Kurdistan. In this role, he promised to "solve" the Kurdish "problem" through slaughter. The Kurds were viewed as a problem in that they desired their own autonomous area, were hard to control, often clashed with Iraqi military forces, and were known to have sided with Iran during the Iran–Iraq War of 1980–88. Al-Majid issued orders for the Kurds to leave their ancestral villages and homes, and to move into camps where they could be scrutinised by the Iraqi government. Those who refused to move from what then became "prohibited zones" were thereafter considered traitors, and targeted for annihilation.

The Iraqi attack, when it came, included gassing the Kurds in their villages and machine-gunning others after they had been captured and taken to remote locations. The campaign, which began in 1987, was codenamed "al-Anfal." In Arabic, the word *Anfal* is used to describe plundering, or carrying the spoils of plunder away; the term's origin is from *Al-Anfal*, the title of the eighth sura ("The Spoils") in the Qur'an. It was an odd choice for a codename: the Kurds, like the Iraqi Arabs, are Muslim. Iraq, moreover, is a secular state. The Iraqi government used the term to provide a religious rationale for its attack on the Kurds.

The campaign continued through 1988, and saw Iraqi troops, military police, and reserve forces of the National Defence Battalions destroy 1,000 or more Iraqi Kurdish villages and kill nearly 200,000 Iraqi Kurds, most of whom were unarmed and many of whom were defenceless women and children (Leezenburg 2013: 395). Those who survived were often forced into areas bereft of water, food, housing, or medical care. The genocide of Iraq's Kurds took place within the space of just six months.

It was here that al-Majid earned his nickname of "Chemical Ali," from the crime for which he was finally convicted: attacks in which he ordered the indiscriminate use of chemical weapons such as mustard gas, sarin, tabun, and VX against Kurdish targets.

Included among those killed were some 5,000 who died in one day when Halabja, a Kurdish town in northern Iraq located about 150 miles north-east of Baghdad, was saturated by chemical weapons on March 16, 1988. This was the largest chemical weapons attack directed against a civilian-populated area in history. For many people, the attack on Halabja is considered to be a separate event from the Anfal genocide, though the destruction took place simultaneously with the broader campaign (Hiltermann 2007).

Al-Majid's willingness to use gas led to international accusations of genocide, accusations that were subsequently verified by numerous independent organisations, such as Human Rights Watch. (After Iraq's defeat in the Gulf War of 1991, Kurds in the north and Shi'ites in the south, specifically the Ma'dan people or "Marsh Arabs," encouraged by US President George H. W. Bush (b. 1924), rebelled against Ba'ath Party rule. Again, al-Majid was in the forefront of the suppression of this resistance.)

Within the US, opposition to Saddam and al-Majid was led by a young Foreign Service officer, Peter Galbraith (b. 1950). In September 1988, Galbraith was sent to the Turkey/Iraq border region to investigate at first hand the condition of Iraqi Kurds who had fled the al-Anfal campaign. Interviewing a large number of survivors, he collected documentation on 49 chemical weapon attacks against Kurdish villagers and concluded that the Iraqi campaign was systematic, state-driven, and genocidal in nature. His report was circulated throughout Congress and the White House, and he sought every opportunity to keep US attention focused on the murderous policies of the Iraqi government (Galbraith 2006).

Back in Washington, Galbraith's work yielded results when the Senate passed a resolution imposing comprehensive sanctions against Iraq later in 1988. He also drafted a bill for an Act of Congress that would be called the Prevention of Genocide Act. It would have imposed the harshest American economic sanctions against any country in 20 years. In achieving this, however, he was unsuccessful. Enormous opposition was generated, principally from those with vested economic interests. Lobbyists warned that the bill would only punish Americans who were doing business with Iraq, and Galbraith found himself facing active resistance from farmers, bankers, exporters, and oil men. Ultimately, the Prevention of Genocide Act was set aside as a result of antagonism from the White House. The government of then-President Ronald Reagan held that sanctions were premature, and Reagan himself hinted that he would be prepared to use his presidential veto to kill the bill if it went ahead. Debate in the House and the Senate stalled the issue until Congress adjourned, and all further discussion of the Prevention of Genocide Act lapsed permanently.

This sent a message to Saddam that the United States was more concerned about the economic implications of action against genocide than about its moral dimensions. His subsequent actions pointed to a belief that he could literally get away with murder. While by this stage the Cold War was in the process of coming to an end, the four-decade-long atmosphere of inaction seemed to have created a knee-jerk response of negativity from the West when faced with a genocidal situation.

OVERALL IMPACT

Generally speaking, the Cold War had a devastating effect on post-1945 hopes that a new, non-genocidal regime could be created across the globe, nowhere more so than in Asia. Not only were those involved in conflict situations left to fight out their differences unimpeded, but all too often, as the democratic West and the communist East saw the possibility of achieving an advantage, those committing genocidal acts were frequently aided and abetted for the most blatant of *realpolitik* motives.

As long as the Cold War continued, there was little chance that the kind of pressures leading to genocide would find a "circuit breaker." The superpowers led the way in manipulating local conflicts in order to suit their own needs, after which each side was able to serve as a proxy in the greater ideological conflicts of the time. The Cold War showed that the world's major players paid only lip service to their post-war commitment to the notion of "Never Again" where genocide was concerned, and the context in which these many tragedies were played out permitted an international culture of immobility. This not only permitted genocide to take place, but also provided precedents for the future, crushing post-war hopes for a genocide-free world.

DISCUSSION QUESTIONS

- To what extent was the Cold War responsible for outbreaks of genocide in Asia during the four decades after 1945?
- Was the creation of Bangladesh in 1971 a direct result of Cold War rivalries?
- Does the United States bear some responsibility for the Cambodian Genocide owing to its actions in that country during the Vietnam War?
- Did the international community fail in East Timor, or were world leaders too distracted during the 1970s and 1980s to enable effective action that could save the people from being massacred by the Indonesians?
- Was Saddam Hussein's campaign against the Kurds genocidal in its intentions?

6

GENOCIDE IN THE 1990s

THE UNITED NATIONS

The primary task of the United Nations is to maintain peace between sovereign member states. Its actions are governed by its Charter, which defines members' rights and obligations, and establishes how the organisation should operate and what its various structures and agencies will be. The Charter codifies the major principles of international relations, from the sovereign equality of states to the prohibition of the use of force in international relations (Meisler 2011). In the UN's General Assembly, each member state is entitled to one vote, and all decisions are decided by a two-thirds majority. In the broad area of genocide, the most important contribution made by the General Assembly was the passage of the Convention on Genocide in 1948.

While the main arena for UN debates is the General Assembly, its recommendations are, for the most part, passed to the Security Council for further deliberation and action. The Security Council is the organisation's most powerful deliberative body, with the authority to make decisions that are binding on member states; in this, it differs from other UN organisations, which can only make recommendations.

The Security Council consists of five permanent members (United States, United Kingdom, France, Russia, and China), and ten temporary members elected for a period of two years, chosen from within designated global regions (Latin America, Asia, Western Europe, Eastern Europe, and Africa; there is, in addition, an Arab delegate that is elected alternately from the Asian or African cohort). The five permanent members possess a power of veto on Security Council votes; if a permanent member vetoes a decision then the resolution will fail, owing to a rule that all votes must be unanimous among the permanent members in order to become operative (Genser and Ugarte 2014).

The Security Council is the branch of the UN most closely identified with **peacekeeping** and peacemaking operations. Its main role is to maintain peace and security between states; its primary means of doing this are to be found in Chapter VI of the Charter, which deals with the settlement of disputes, and Chapter VII, which covers the prospect of armed intervention in order to stop aggression or to defend the victims of attack. During the 1990s, the tension between Chapter VI and Chapter VII saw a number of unsuccessful peacekeeping initiatives that resulted in fiascos that neither saved lives nor brought peace.

PEACEKEEPING

All UN peacekeeping operations are established by the Security Council, and directed by the United Nations Secretary-General through a Special Representative. When a military mission is sent to enforce or monitor a peacekeeping mission, the senior military officer is designated either as the Force Commander or as the Chief Military Observer; this person is then responsible for all military and day-to-day aspects of the operation.

The United Nations' Department of Peacekeeping Operations, or DPKO, is the agency responsible for all peacekeeping, peace-making, peace enforcement, and related actions. Its chief officer is the Under-Secretary-General for Peacekeeping Operations. In view of the fact that the United Nations does not have its own military force, it must depend on member states to volunteer the personnel and equipment needed for all operations (Bellamy and Williams 2013). Peacekeepers continue to wear their own state's military uniform, but are identified as UN peacekeepers by a blue helmet or beret.

Peacekeeping operations take many shapes and forms, and can be activated in order to undertake a variety of different tasks. These include the implementation of peace settlements, the maintenance of ceasefires, and the protection of humanitarian operations.

Peace enforcement missions see troops armed with a Chapter VII mandate, in which case they are authorised to employ deadly force, if necessary, to achieve their objectives of saving the lives of non-combatants.

Coming immediately after the collapse of communism, the 1990s posed an enormous challenge for the United Nations. The Cold War had had a devastating effect on post-1945 hopes that a world without genocide could be created. Not only were warring groups left to fight out their differences unimpeded, but all too often, as democratic and communist states vied with each other in the quest to achieve an advantage, those committing violent acts were aided and abetted by the Great Powers for the most blatant of *realpolitik* motives.

After the Cold War, however, the record of the international community preventing genocide was even worse, despite the fact – paradoxically – that the United Nations engaged in more acts of humanitarian intervention throughout the 1990s and early 2000s than at any other time in history (Fleitz 2002).

When the Cold War came to an end, hopes that a new period of peace had arrived mirrored the optimistic feelings of 1945, though this was short-lived. The previously suppressed internal tensions that had been held back by the Cold War now erupted in violent conflicts in the Middle East, in Europe, and in Africa. In response, the international community, no longer prevented by the tension between the USSR and the USA that had earlier inhibited inter-vention, saw the chance to keep, enforce, or make peace. Only very rarely, however, was this successful.

BOSNIA

The disaster of Bosnia-Herzegovina, in the former Yugoslavia, dominated international news for much of the 1990s. It was the first occasion since the Holocaust that people claimed genocide was taking place within a military conflict in Europe. It involved the killing and displacement of Bosnia's Muslims (known as Bosniaks) by Bosnian Serbs and Serbian forces from the Yugoslav People's Army (*Jugoslovenska Narodna Armija*, or JNA). These actions were justified by the perpetrators on the grounds of ideology and the need to acquire (or retain) territory for Serbia. The questions thrown up by the conflict were many, but, in a world climate that had pledged after the Holocaust that such a phenomenon would never again be permitted to happen, efforts to stop genocide in Bosnia while it was happening were neither quick to emerge nor, when they did, effective.

Bosnia-Herzegovina was, and remains, a much-disputed region. The Romans, Byzantines, Ottomans, and Habsburgs all sought to gain control of this strategic Balkan territory, and all left their mark, especially in the form of a multi-ethnic population consisting of Croats (Catholics), Serbs (Orthodox), and Muslim Bosniaks.

During the Second World War, some Bosniaks collaborated with the Croatian fascist *Ustashe* in the formation of a Nazi puppet state called Greater Croatia, accompanied by anti-Serb persecution and mass murder. The memory of this was not lost on future generations, especially when Yugoslavia began to disintegrate in the early 1990s.

Under the communist regime of Marshal Josip Broz Tito (1892–1980), Bosnia-Herzegovina became the heartland of Yugoslavia's military industries, whose engineers and managers were largely drawn from the urban Bosniak population rather than from the more rural Croats and Serbs (Malcolm 1996). At the same time, Bosnia's diverse population became the most ethnically integrated of all the Yugoslav republics, though this was not enough to stem the tide of hostile ethnonationalism, especially when it was whipped up by Serbia's and Croatia's leaders, Slobodan Milošević (1941–2006) and Franjo Tudjman (1922–99).

The war for the partition of Bosnia was fought so ferociously that it became a three-way war of atrocities and counter-atrocities involving Milošević, Tudjman, and Bosnian President Alija Izetbegović (1925–2004). This vicious, fratricidal warfare resulted in the death of up to 100,000 Bosnians (Mennecke 2013: 478).

Characterising the conflict was the introduction of policies of what became known as "**ethnic cleansing**," a term employed to describe attempts to force minorities off their land. The many offensives to drive people out intensified with the formation of paramilitary militia units; while the end goal was the "liberation" of land from its "alien" inhabitants, an increasing emphasis was placed on killing as a means to ensure that those displaced would never return (Naimark 2001; Bell-Fialkoff 1999). Ethnic cleansing of non-Serb populations became the norm rather than the exception, and was coupled with the physical destruction of cultural and religious sites.

Typically, the process would begin with the harassment of local citizens, who would be intimidated, often in fear of their lives, to leave their homes. Such terror, with variations, included torture, rape, beatings, and mutilation, and extended to murder. Once an area had been "cleansed" of its unwanted population, the perpetrators moved in their own people, and altered the character of the region as though the original owners had never been there in the first place. In this way, they laid claim to the region as of right, with no-one able to claim pre-existing title through prior occupation.

Particularly during 1992 and 1993, Serbian forces were also known to commit mass rapes against Bosniak and Croat women in officially created "rape camps." As mass rape became institutionalised, groups of women would be enslaved in ethnically cleansed schools, homes, restaurants, and other places which served as brothels for the Serb fighters (Allen 1996). There were two essential reasons behind this strategy. The first was to add to the climate of fear, encouraging the flight of Bosniaks from towns and villages; as such, it put all women on notice that if they did not leave they could be subject to rape (Stiglmayer 1994).

The second reason was to introduce rape as an instrument of genocide. Bosniak women of child-bearing age were systematically subjected to repeated rape in order to destroy their ethnic identity; by virtue of their ordeal, they would be socially ostracised upon returning to their original communities. They could never be married, and those already married could be divorced. Their rape created permanent stigma, pushing them to the fringes of society and transforming them into pariahs. Were they to fall pregnant – an objective of the rapes, in many cases – they would be doubly "tainted" upon returning home. Children born of the rape would be perceived as of mixed ethnicity, and not as a member of the community into which they were born (Allen 1996).

The central idea behind the mass rapes was thus to weaken the fabric of the Bosniaks as a group, and, in that sense, mass rape was part of a genocidal campaign (Rittner and Roth 2012). Not only this, as by rendering their victims "untouchable" and unfit for marriage within Bosniak society, the Serbs were also reducing the available pool of women from whom the next generation would be born. While increasing the number of Serb children, the rapes were also reducing the number of Bosniak children in the future.

By way of response to the Serbs' ethnic cleansing operations, the United Nations established a number of what it referred to as "**safe areas**" during the conflict, an initiative that had a longer history in UN operations (Shelton 2004: 939–942). UN humanitarian relief efforts to deliver food, medical supplies, and the like were, however, constantly hampered by Serb interference with aid convoys. Frequently, the safe areas became little more than besieged towns and cities that were poorly guarded by UN troops with inadequate mandates.

On February 21, 1992 the United Nations authorised, by Security Council Resolution 743, the creation of what became known as the United Nations Protection Force, or UNPROFOR. Its mission underwent change from the moment of its founding (before the war in Bosnia began), but by June 1992 the mandate was extended to ensure that the safe areas were demilitarised and their inhabitants were safe from armed attack. UNPROFOR was also authorised to use military force in self-defence, and to coordinate with NATO on the use of airpower support. By November 30, 1994, 37 nation states had supplied approximately 39,000 military, civilian police personnel, and observers (Totten and Bartrop 2008: 442).

The safe areas were established as places where local Bosniaks, as well as those from other parts of the country, could live in relative safety. As a result of various UN resolutions between April and May 1993, Srebrenica, Sarajevo, Tuzla, Žepa, Goražde, and Bihać were all designated as safe areas, to be supervised and guarded by troops from UNPROFOR. They were, however, often shelled by Serb forces, with UNPROFOR peacekeepers frequently threatened and, on occasion, attacked.

The most egregious breach of the safe areas took place on July 11, 1995, when Serb forces attacked the safe area of Srebrenica (Rohde 1997; Honig and Both 1997). A small city in eastern Bosnia, Srebrenica became the scene of the greatest single massacre on European soil since the Holocaust. It was declared a UN safe area on April 16, 1993, but it constantly suffered privation as Serb forces persisted in blocking UN aid convoys. Srebrenica became a symbol of Bosniak resistance, but, on July 6, 1995, its defiance came to an end. Encouraged by UN equivocation over whether or not to maintain the safe areas initiative, Bosnian Serb General Ratko Mladić (b. 1942) led a ten-day campaign to take Srebrenica and subject it to ethnic cleansing.

As the campaign was getting underway, thousands of Srebrenica's men and boys fled the city in order to reach Bosnian forces beyond the hills, presumably hoping to lead them back to defend the city. The women, children, and elderly were for the most part loaded onto Serb-chartered buses and evacuated. Upon taking the city, and overrunning the UNPROFOR base at nearby Potočari, Mladić's men began hunting down the Bosniak men who were then struggling through Serb-controlled lines. Capturing them in small groups, the Serbs concentrated them in larger numbers in fields, sports grounds, schools, and factories, where they were slaughtered in their thousands. It is impossible to arrive at anything but an approximation of the number murdered as many mass graves are still yet to be located, and population figures from before the fall of the city are imprecise owing to the large number of uncounted refugees who had earlier flooded into the city. Best estimates have fluctuated between 7,500 and 8,000 killed (Rohde 1997; Horvitz and Catherwood 2006: 402).

Srebrenica epitomised the brutality of the Serb war against the Bosniaks, as well as of the UN's failure to stand up to genocide – especially given the fact that the safe zone was not defended, but simply allowed to be taken with the connivance and assent of the Dutch peacekeepers and their NATO commanders. This needs to be examined in greater depth.

In late January 1994, the first units of a 1,170-strong Dutch paratroop battalion (codenamed "Dutchbat") were deployed to Bosnia, and, on March 3, some 570 of their number entered Srebrenica to relieve a much smaller Canadian detachment. In the 16 months that followed, Dutchbat experienced a range of challenging situations, including military deaths in combat conditions, and the capture of some of its soldiers and subsequent abuse by Bosnian Serb forces as human shields.

During the takeover of the city in July 1995, the Serb troops separated men and boys from their wives, mothers, and sisters. Some allegations have asserted that, far from being passive bystanders, the officers of Dutchbat were active participants in the genocide, even to the extent of assisting people onto the buses that would take them out of the city in the ethnic cleansing process (Nuhanović 2007).

When news of the attack arrived in the Netherlands, a great deal of national soul-searching followed. Dutch citizens were dismayed when it became known that, the night before the final Serb assault on the city, the Dutchbat commander, Lieutenant-Colonel Tom Karremans (b. 1949), had drunk a toast with General Mladić – in honour, it was said, of Mladić's victory. (Karremans later explained that it was only a glass of water, but by then, courtesy of Serb photographers filming the exchange, the damage had been done.) The fall of Srebrenica, and the death of its citizens by the thousands, was seen as a matter of national shame in the Netherlands.

In 1996, the Dutch government of Prime Minister Wim Kok (b. 1938) commissioned an official inquiry into the actions of the peacekeepers, and its report was issued on April 10, 2002. Six days later the entire Dutch government resigned, followed immediately by the Army Chief of Staff, General Ad van Baal (b. 1947).

The role of the Dutch peacekeepers at Srebrenica was at the least ineffectual; at most, it was criminal in its complicity with the Bosnian Serbs (Nuhanović 2007). What it pointed to most clearly was the danger to be found in UN security operations that were not sufficiently supported at every level, and arguments were put that Dutchbat's mandate was not clear enough, nor the troops properly trained or equipped, for the tasks they were required to undertake. They were, in short, sent on a mission to keep the peace where there was no peace to keep.

As if to underscore the failure of the safe havens initiative and the impotence of the UN in Bosnia, a second safe area, Žepa, was overrun on July 25, 1995. The Ukrainian peacekeepers there proved to be just as inadequate in this instance as the forces of Dutchbat had been at Srebrenica.

In early 1995 a British general, Sir Rupert Smith (b.1943), was appointed as UNPROFOR commander, replacing another British general, Sir Michael Rose (b. 1940). Smith's arrival appeared to signal an immediate change of mood. He was determined to break the cycle of what he saw as appeasement of the Serbs, vulnerability of the Bosniak civilians, and inaction on the part of UNPROFOR – features that seemed to have characterised the mission from the start. Smith proceeded to fulfil his mandate by militarily deterring attacks on the UN safe areas and ensuring the passage of humanitarian aid – and, where necessary, using the armed force permitted him under Chapter VII of the UN Charter.

The response saw much more intensive deployment of NATO air power than before, and the use of wide-ranging air strikes targeting Serb command and control centres. Smith used the same strategy to break the siege of Sarajevo, and created a UN rapid reaction force to ensure the Serbs complied with the new circumstances. In May 1995, Smith destroyed two Bosnian Serb ammunition dumps at Pale, bringing the war home as closely as possible to Bosnian Serb President Radovan Karadžić (b. 1945) (Bartrop 2012: 301–303).

It was through actions such as these that the military reality facing the Bosnian Serbs became clear, and, as a result, a set of steps began that would ultimately lead to a peace settlement by November 1995.

An interim peace agreement was signed at the Wright-Patterson Air Force Base, near Dayton, Ohio, on November 21, 1995. As a summit meeting involving heads of states and other leading figures, the peace conference was officially hosted by the President of the United States, Bill Clinton (b. 1946), though it was chaired by Clinton's principal Balkans negotiator, Richard Holbrooke (1941–2010). The major negotiators were Serbia's Milošević, Croatia's Tudjman, and Bosnia's Izetbegović. Other participants included senior military figures from the United States, the United Kingdom, France, and Germany.

The subsequent full and final agreement took place in Paris, on December 14, 1995. This was again signed by Milošević, Tudjman, and Izetbegović, but not they alone: in a pledge to safeguard the peace thus created, the Paris Protocol was also signed by Clinton, British Prime Minister John Major (b. 1943), French President Jacques Chirac (b. 1932), German Chancellor Helmut Kohl (b. 1930), and Russian Prime Minister Viktor Chernomyrdin (1938–2010).

The two agreements, though bringing peace, were controversial. They appeared to reward the Bosnian Serbs territorially for having engaged in ethnic cleansing. Because of this, Holbrooke, the major architect of the settlement, was later to maintain that he had no qualms about negotiating with killers, if it meant that by doing so he could prevent the death of people still alive (Holbrooke 1998).

The genocide in Bosnia – though probably the most closely reported in history – was yet another case of international inaction in the face of massive human rights violations. In Bosnia, the Western powers, led by the UN, the European Community, and NATO, failed consistently both to resolve the war and to stop the killing.

RWANDA

While the Bosnian War was taking place, the international community was confronted by another genocidal conflict of even more immediate urgency, this time in Africa, and in one of the smallest countries in the world.

In the Central African country of Rwanda, between April and July, 1994, genocide was committed against Tutsi and liberal democratic, or "moderate," Hutu by the extremist Hutu Power regime of the ruling *Mouvement Révolutionnaire Nationale pour le Développement* (National Revolutionary Movement for Development, or MRND).

Traditionally, Hutu life was founded on a clan basis in which small kingdoms prevailed, but, after the arrival of the Tutsi in the fifteenth century, a feudal system was established in which the Hutu were reduced to vassal status and were ruled over by a Tutsi aristocracy headed by a king (*mwaami*). The fundamental division between Hutu and Tutsi was based more on a form of class difference than on ethnicity, particularly as a great deal of intermarriage took place.

Though the actual genocide lasted a mere 100 days, the three murderous months had a long background tracing back to the German and Belgian colonial period (1893 to 1962), when Hutu and Tutsi were identified as distinctly different peoples, with the Tutsi accorded a higher social and ethnic status than the majority Hutu. Under Belgian colonial rule in Rwanda, identity cards bearing an individual's ethnic group were introduced in 1933. Not only the ethnic background, but also the bearer's place of residence was recorded on these cards, and the person in whose name the card was held could not relocate to another address without approval from the colonial authorities. After Rwanda's independence in 1962, the identity cards were retained as a means of positive discrimination in favour of the Hutu majority (Prunier 1997; Totten and Bartrop 2008: 202–203).

While the relationship between the Hutu and their neighbours prior to the 1950s had essentially been based on hierarchy and dominance, Hutu–Tutsi relationships were, for the most part, relatively peaceful. After Rwanda's independence from Belgium in 1962, however, frequent Hutu persecutions of Tutsi took place, with the end of colonial rule overturning the earlier ranking of peoples, and an ethnic radicalisation of the Hutu seeing them claim their rights as a majority for the first time. This triggered periodic outbursts of escalating violence in 1962 and 1973, following an earlier pogrom in 1959, before independence. By the early 1990s, extensive and somewhat transparent plans were laid to carry out a campaign of extermination of the Tutsi and their moderate Hutu political allies.

Instrumental in preparing the Hutu population for the genocide to follow was the creation of anti-Tutsi militias. The *Interahamwe* (Kinyarwanda, "those who stick together"), was the largest and most important of these. The movement's genesis could be found in a number of junior soccer clubs, one of which, the *Loisirs* ("Leisure") club, was coached by Robert "Jerry" Kajuga (b. 1960). Under his direction, the *Interahamwe* was transformed from a youth organisation when it was founded in 1990 into a radical Hutu killing machine (Totten and Bartrop 2008: 237). Originally trained by the French at the request of Rwandan President Juvénal Habyarimana (1937–94), the *Interahamwe* would form the shock troops of the Hutu war of extermination.

In the pre-genocide years, the *Interahamwe* engaged in lethal street fights hoping to upset the social order. Their weapons were provided by the army, allowing them to engage in daily murder sprees employing machetes and other implements. When the call for action finally came after Habyarimana's assassination on April 6, 1994, none were more bloodthirsty or ready for action than the *Interahamwe*.

From this time on, *Interahamwe* killing units were left to their own devices; they were merciless in their devotion to what they saw as their racial duty, as were the other killing factions such as the *Impuzamugambi* (Kinyarwanda, "those with a single purpose"), another anti-Tutsi extremist militia that worked closely with the *Interahamwe* (though the members of each remained conscious of their separate political identities). What is most significant about the existence of these militias is that they showed the genocide to be far from spontaneous but, instead, a carefully planned campaign of extermination that had its executioners prepared and waiting to go into action long before the killing actually began (Des Forges 1999).

Opposition came in the form of an organisation called the Rwandan Patriotic Front (RPF), established in Uganda in 1985 by Tutsi refugees who had grown to maturity since their parents had been exiled in earlier anti-Tutsi pogroms. By 1992, under Paul Kagame (b. 1957), the RPF was a large military force of well-trained soldiers. Faced with a formidable potential enemy, and in a situation where substantial fighting had already begun in some places, the Rwandan government had signed a peace settlement with the RPF at Arusha, Tanzania, on August 4, 1992.

The Arusha Accords were a set of five agreements negotiated with the intention of ending this nascent civil war. The talks had been co-sponsored by the United States, France, and the Organisation of African Unity, and ranged over a wide variety of topics: refugee resettlement, power sharing between Hutu and Tutsi, the introduction of an all-embracing democratic regime, the dismantling of the military **dictatorship** of President Habyarimana, and the encouragement of a transparent rule of law. In the months that followed, a number of subsequent meetings took place for the purpose of facilitating their implementation. This involved the parties travelling to and from Arusha, sometimes by road and at other times by plane. It was after one of these meetings, on April 6, 1994, that the plane carrying Habyarimana and the President of Burundi, Cyprien Ntaryamira (1955–94), was shot down – it has never been proven conclusively by whom – by a missile fired from the outskirts of Kigali airport. All on board were killed, triggering the genocide.

Earlier, on October 5, 1993 the UN Security Council, by Resolution 872, had established UNAMIR, the United Nations Assistance Mission for (often inaccurately, "in") Rwanda, for the express purpose of helping to implement the Arusha Accords.

A Canadian artillery officer, Lieutenant-General Roméo Dallaire (b. 1946), was named as Force Commander. His mission's mandate included monitoring the ceasefire agreement; providing security for the Rwandan capital city of Kigali; monitoring the security situation during the final period of the transitional government's mandate leading up to elections; and assisting in the coordination of humanitarian assistance activities. It was Dallaire's first UN command, and for most of those involved it was anticipated that this would be a relatively straightforward mission (Dallaire with Beardsley 2003).

A reality to which Dallaire was not alerted prior to his posting was that extremist Hutu were intent on annihilating the Tutsi, and had said as much in media broadcasts, newspaper articles, and declarations. Dallaire's first major test – apart from trying to ensure that his force was equipped and ready to carry out its mission despite an appalling lag time in the transfer of *matériel* from donor countries – came in early 1994.

On January 10, Dallaire received intelligence that a radical Hutu, codenamed "Jean-Pierre," was prepared to disclose information regarding a planned genocide of Tutsi. Jean-Pierre had been an officer in Rwanda's Presidential Guard, but had left to become one of the key men in the *Interahamwe*. He described in detail how the *Interahamwe* were trained, by whom, and where, adding that the militia was in a state of permanent readiness sufficient to kill 1,000 Tutsi in Kigali within 20 minutes of receiving an order to do so. As a sign of his goodwill, Jean-Pierre offered to reveal the location of a large stockpile of weapons somewhere in central Kigali. Dallaire, operating within the terms of his mandate, assessed that these arms had to be confiscated. He decided to order an arms raid, and faxed the UN Department of Peacekeeping Operations in New York, headed at that time by Kofi Annan (b. 1938), for authorisation. This cable outlined in detail Jean-Pierre's revelations.

Dallaire's request was denied, and DPKO ordered him not to carry out the raid. He was ordered to turn over to President Habyarimana – the very man whose anti-Tutsi cause the *Interahamwe* was enforcing – what Jean-Pierre had disclosed. The Department of Peacekeeping Operations, together with the office of Secretary-General Boutros Boutros-Ghali (b. 1922), decided that process was more important than action; not only this, but they were concerned for the image of the UN in light of an earlier failed arms raid that took place with heavy loss of life in Mogadishu, Somalia, in October, 1993. Dallaire protested the decision insistently, but New York would not budge, with catastrophic consequences three months later (Dallaire with Beardsley 2003).

As the crisis in Rwanda worsened, particularly in early 1994, Dallaire concluded that the constant stream of murders he and his soldiers were witnessing was not a result of warfare between two combatants, but, rather, of crimes against humanity by one group against another. He sent one urgent message after another to UN headquarters requesting more forces and supplies, and the broadening of his mandate to quell the violence, but it was all to no avail.

The climate of violence was far from eased by a constant barrage of intense anti-Tutsi propaganda broadcast over *Radio-Télévision Libre des Mille Collines* (RTLM) and through the pages of the newspaper *Kangura*. RTLM was an independent radio station that operated from July 8, 1993 until it shut down on July 31, 1994. Established as Rwanda's first non-government radio station, it became a primary instrument in the preparation and execution of the genocide. RTLM had a greater degree of freedom in spreading its anti-Tutsi message than did the state broadcaster, Radio Rwanda.

Months before the outbreak of violence in April 1994, RTLM was broadcasting a carefully prepared daily regimen aimed at demonising the Tutsi minority. Day by day the rhetoric escalated as a vocabulary of genocide was introduced, and mental images of Tutsi as "cockroaches" (*Inyenzi*) intensified the emotional content of the hate programmes it broadcast. This allowed radicals both in and outside the government to reach into every corner of the land and inflame the Hutu against their Tutsi neighbours.

The total absence of any counter-propaganda added to RTLM's effectiveness. The voices of hatred maintained their broadcasts uninterrupted throughout the three months of the genocide, fuelling the frenzied killing and announcing to a nationwide audience the location of Tutsi and Tutsi sympathisers, with the command that they be murdered immediately (Temple-Raston 2008).

Kangura, which could be counted as the print version of RTLM, was an anti-Tutsi newspaper that first appeared in May, 1990. It ceased publication in February, 1994 – two months before the genocide began. In Kinyarwanda, the word *Kangura* translates as "wake them up," and it constantly sought to do so for the Hutu population. Perhaps its most infamous piece was the "Hutu Ten Commandments," a series of instructions that were to be followed by every Hutu in order to destroy Tutsi influence (Totten and Bartrop 2008: 200–201). These could in many respects have been adapted directly out of the Nazi Nuremberg Laws, and their constant repetition served as a conditioning agent for the Hutu against the Tutsi.

Elsewhere, *Kangura* published material that drove home the message that the Tutsi were about to enslave all the Hutu and/or exterminate them. The answer, it put rhetorically (and frequently), was to pre-empt the Tutsi and wipe them out. Prior to ceasing publication, *Kangura* also published the names of Hutu deemed to be politically suspect – insinuating that they should suffer the same fate as the Tutsi – and exhorted all other Hutu to take measures to ensure that they would predominate now and into the future (Thompson 2007).

The final event precipitating genocide was the death of President Habyarimana on April 6, 1994. His assassination acted as a signal for radical Hutu across the country to commence their long-planned operation. Within two hours, roadblocks were erected in many parts of Kigali. These stopped the traffic flow, at which point occupants of cars, trucks, and buses were required to present their identity cards to the Hutu militias. If the identity card showed the bearer as a Tutsi, immediate and summary execution by machetes, clubs, or (less frequently) gunfire would most often follow. The construction of these roadblocks had been carefully planned and coordinated some time beforehand, and was further evidence of the pre-meditated nature of the genocide.

Fighting broke out immediately, and genocidal mass murder began against the Tutsi and any Hutu who opposed the killers. The first to be targeted were Hutu officials identified with opposition parties (and therefore seen to hold pro-RPF sympathies). Opposition figures, both Hutu and Tutsi, were disposed of in a matter of hours. Within a day, ten of Dallaire's peacekeepers from Belgium had been murdered while trying to protect the interim head of state, Prime Minister Agathe Uwilingiyimana (1953–94), but she, too, was murdered. Dallaire's immediate conclusion was that UNAMIR's mandate was now untenable in light of the changed circumstances, but despite his repeated pleas for a stronger Chapter VII mandate and more troops and arms, which would have allowed UNAMIR to engage the *génocidaires* in combat, the UN steadfastly refused to provide him with additional troops.

The scale and speed of the massacres left no doubt about the determination of the machete-wielding militias. A major feature of the killings was the manner in which they took place. The interim government exhorted *every* Hutu to kill Tutsi, wherever they could be found, as mass murder became transformed into a civic virtue. For weeks and months, from one locality after another, hundreds and thousands of Tutsi civilians were shot, speared, clubbed, or hacked to pieces in their homes, churches, and schools. That carnage of this magnitude could have been going on day after day, week after week, without interference from the international community speaks volumes for its lack of resolve in dealing with these atrocities (Power 2002; Melvern 2000; Melvern 2004; Wallis 2007; Cameron 2013).

Dallaire pleaded for UNAMIR to be immediately reinforced. He put forth a plan arguing that, with an overall command of 5,000 well-equipped and highly trained troops, he could stop the killing and re-impose peace. The Security Council refused, and then dropped a bombshell of its own: on April 21 it voted to reduce UNAMIR, justifying its decision by saying that the mission to monitor the peace was now redundant. With this change, Dallaire's mission was reduced from 2,548 to 270 personnel, and Dallaire was ordered home. He, together with his Deputy Force Commander, General Henry Kwami Anyidoho (b. 1940) of Ghana, and ably supported by his Chief of Staff, Major Brent Beardsley (b. 1954), refused to obey. Stripped of authority, manpower, resources, and logistical support, Dallaire and what remained of UNAMIR did what they could to help people, Dallaire's intervention alone saving an estimated 30,000 Tutsi and moderate Hutu in safe areas such as the Amahoro Stadium and the Mille Collines Hotel (Dallaire with Beardsley 2003).

The killing continued, however. Ultimately, the Security Council revised its earlier decision and, too late, voted to establish a revamped mission, UNAMIR II, with a troop complement of 5,500. It did not arrive until early July, however, after the genocide had ended with the victory of the RPF under General Kagame. By that stage, estimates range between 800,000 and one million murdered in the space of 100 days (Des Forges 1999; Prunier 1997). Were it not for the armed intervention of the RPF, the genocide might well have been total.

On July 18, 1994, the RPF took power in Kigali. Its victory and the new government were promptly recognised by the international community. On July 19, Pasteur Bizimungu (b. 1950), a Hutu member of the RPF, was proclaimed as Rwanda's new President, and Faustin Twagiramungu (b. 1945), also a Hutu, as Prime Minister of a national unity government. Paul Kagame was named as Vice-President.

KOSOVO

In the aftermath of the drawn-out and bloody conflict in Bosnia-Herzegovina between 1992 and 1995, Serbia's nationalist regime, led by Slobodan Milošević, seemed at first to settle down and return to the world of peaceable nations. In March, 1998, however, violence once more erupted, this time in Serbia itself – or, more specifically, in its southern province of Kosovo. The long-term ethnic and religious animosity in the province between minority Serbs and majority Kosovars (a Muslim people of Albanian ethnicity) led to the establishment of a self-defence organisation, the Kosovo Liberation Army (KLA), which engaged in terrorist activities in order to attract international attention to their cause and at the same time intimidate Serbs in the province to leave Kosovo.

The KLA was an underground movement created in the late 1990s to resist Milošević's plan to evict the Albanian majority from Kosovo. At first it was comprised of several hundred radical Kosovar secessionists who opposed the more moderate majority, led by their Prime Minister-in-waiting, Ibrahim Rugova (1944–2006), who sought instead to achieve compromise. The KLA rejected this as utopian in light of the bloody events in Bosnia between 1992 and 1995.

As tension intensified, a carefully planned operation carried out by the KLA on January 8, 1999 ambushed and killed three Serbian policemen. Another was murdered two days later. In response, on January 15, Serb police and army detachments attacked the village of Račak, in south-western Kosovo. Army artillery had already hit the town in the days leading up to the assault, and with the advance into Račak a large number of men and boys – at least 45, but possibly more – were butchered by the Serb forces. One was a boy aged 12; two were women; one of the men was decapitated (Totten and Bartrop 2008: 350–351). US Ambassador William Walker (b. 1935), the head of the UN's Kosovo Verification Mission monitoring Serb progress towards an easing of conditions for Kosovar Albanians, immediately condemned the massacre as the work of Serbs, and declared the victims to be innocent civilians.

Based largely on Walker's assessment, but confirmed by other eyewitness accounts, world leaders quickly came to the conclusion that the situation existing in Kosovo had to be changed permanently. US Secretary of State Madeleine Albright (b. 1937) realised that any attempts at negotiation with the Serbs had to be backed by a credible threat of force, and that NATO had to be the major vehicle for enforcing it.

Račak, as a catalyst for military intervention, had one further implication: an attempt at ethnic cleansing by Serb forces acting on Milošević's orders. Increasingly, the United States and its European allies saw a need to intervene before this state-initiated killing got out of hand.

One last chance for peace took place via a series of negotiations involving delegates from the United States, several European NATO countries including Britain, France, and Germany, together with Russia, Yugoslavia, and representatives of Kosovar Albanian groups. These negotiations took place at Rambouillet, near Paris, between February 6 and March 19, 1999. The meeting happened under the shadow of NATO threats of military action in the event of an agreement not being made, but the very fact of getting everyone to a conference table was at first held to be a positive step. The intention was to hammer out a settlement that would be acceptable to all parties, and would avoid the possibility of more bloodshed.

Despite this initial optimism, the negotiations foundered over points that were ultimately unacceptable to one or other of the parties. The Kosovar Albanian delegates – who were disadvantaged by the fact that the groups they represented were still in the field fighting, and out of regular contact with Paris – were absolutely unwilling to negotiate on anything that did not have an independent Kosovo as its end. The Serbs, who saw Kosovo as a Serbian spiritual and nationalist heartland, would not countenance the possibility of Kosovar autonomy (and even less independence), nor would they accept any international interference in Serbia's internal affairs. Both sides wanted their way, but neither was prepared to allow their negotiating position to be held as responsible for the failure of the talks.

Breaking through the impasse seemed impossible, until Albright provided each side with a single option: in response to a set of demands presented by NATO, if one party agreed but the other did not, NATO would support the agreeing party. If Serbia agreed but the Kosovars did not, NATO would withdraw its support of them and walk away, allowing the Serbs full rein to do as they pleased. If the Kosovars agreed but the Serbs did not, NATO would commence military operations against Serbia in order to physically remove their forces from Kosovo. The latter scenario prevailed; NATO action began six days after the talks broke down, on March 25, 1999.

The hope was that this would coerce Milošević into stopping the attacks against the Kosovars, but the opposite took place: rather than succumbing, he took the chance afforded by NATO's intervention to attempt to ethnically cleanse Kosovo of Albanians. Serbian military and paramilitary forces then initiated another round of ethnic cleansing. Within days, between 800,000 and 900,000 were physically expelled, crossing into Macedonia and Albania (Naimark 2001: 180). Thousands were killed, raped, and maimed in the process, and it is from these actions that accusations of genocide have their roots.

The attacks were halted by NATO bombings of Serb positions over the next 77 days, first in Kosovo and then in Serbia itself. The aftermath, in which Milošević surrendered the province, saw the insertion of UN peacekeepers, allowing the refugees to return (Daalder and O'Hanlon 2001). Under cover of the UN, the KLA then waged its own war, seeking to expel Serbs, Roma, and non-Albanian Muslims from Kosovo. Repeated calls from the UN troops for the KLA to disarm and disband were, for a long time, defiantly ignored. Instead, the KLA continued to "cleanse" Kosovo of its ethnic minorities (Judah 2002; Judah 2008: 93).

The Kosovo intervention of 1999 came almost as an acknowledgment of the West's guilty conscience concerning the failure to act earlier, in Bosnia. Now, the air forces of the United States, Britain, France, Germany, Italy, and the Netherlands, operating jointly, attacked Serbia with the intention of forcing the Serbs to stop their persecution of the Kosovar Albanians. It was the first occasion in which a war was fought for the express purpose of stopping genocide before its worst horrors took place. Under international law, the attack was illegal; it was neither called for nor approved by the United Nations. Nonetheless, it was highly successful. The Serbian regime of Milošević, after an intensive bombing campaign, pulled its troops out of Kosovo. The intervention brings up a number of additional questions concerning the role of outsiders facing a genocidal situation, and can be viewed as a case of how a perceived potential genocide can be stopped if the international will to do so exists (Daalder and O'Hanlon 2001).

EAST TIMOR REDUX

In 1998, President Suharto of Indonesia retired after more than three decades in office, and his successor, B.J. Habibie (b. 1936), made it clear that East Timorese independence was out of the question. Then, in January 1999, in a complete turnaround, he announced that a referendum would be held on East Timor's future status. The quarter-century of Indonesian oppression under Suharto's rule had transformed the life of the territory, and Habibie thought that sufficient integration had taken place that the referendum, to be held on August 30, 1999, would vote in Indonesia's favour. It was agreed that the referendum would be overseen by the UN through a monitoring force, UNAMET (United Nations Mission in East Timor), which would organise and conduct a thorough consultation with the people of the territory on the basis of a direct, secret, and universal ballot (Ballard 2007).

Habibie's move made him extremely unpopular with ABRI (*Angkatan Bersenjata Republik Indonesia*), the Indonesian armed forces. Local pro-Indonesian militia groups were established to stop voter registration through a campaign of intimidation, with the aim of ensuring a low turnout on referendum day.

On August 30, 1999, after registration, the people of East Timor cast their votes. The campaign of intimidation and violence to stop voter registration had been unsuccessful. On election day, the turnout was estimated to be 86 per cent. Those agreeing to remain within Indonesia numbered 94,388 (21.5 per cent), with 344,580 (78.5 per cent) voting for independence (http://www.un.org/News/Press/docs/1999/19990903.sc6721.html).

In response, the pro-Indonesian militias went on a rampage. Approximately 1,500 East Timorese were killed and at least 300,000 were forcibly relocated into military-controlled camps in Indonesian-controlled West Timor. Hundreds of women and girls were raped. The majority of the country's infrastructure, including homes, irrigation systems, water supply systems, schools, and the country's entire electrical grid were destroyed. The capital city, Dili, was effectively burned to the ground (Nevins 2005: 95–112). To observers around the world, it seemed as though this was revisiting earlier horrors, during which the world watched ethnic cleansing, mass murder, machetes in the streets, and – many feared – yet another case of genocide in the making (Robinson 2010: 161–184).

The killing and destruction only came to an end once international peacekeepers intervened to halt the violence and place East Timor under United Nations rule on September 20, 1999, some three weeks after the election. UNAMET had been an unarmed force, without a mandate to intervene in the violence accompanying the voting. After some initial hesitation, Australian Prime Minister John Howard (b. 1939) realised that Australia had an obligation to try to ensure that peace and stability should prevail in the region. As a result, Australia and the United States pushed the United Nations to intervene militarily to stop the killing and restore order in the territory, and soon a 9,000-strong multinational force, INTERFET (International Force in East Timor), equipped with a Chapter VII mandate, was assembled and sent to the island (Ballard 2007).

The largest one-off deployment of Australian combat troops since the Second World War (Australia had had a vastly greater number of troops in Vietnam, but these were continually reinforced and built up over time), INTERFET was a multilateral force involving 22 countries in all. The mission was successful in establishing peace and security through a credible and deterrent presence throughout the country. INTERFET's tasks included reconstruction activities following the destruction caused by the militias; assistance with administration; policing and law and order functions; and detection and investigation into allegations of human rights violations (Ballard 2007; Fernandes 2005).

INTERFET remained active in East Timor until February 2000, when its operations gave way to the United Nations Transitional Administration in East Timor, or UNTAET. The purpose of this latter body was to administer the territory and exercise legislative and executive authority during the transition period leading up to East Timor's independence on May 20, 2002.

There can be little doubt that, had the international community not intervened when it did, thousands more innocent victims would have been slaughtered. International intervention, in this case, had been successful in stopping violence and bringing about a peaceful solution – one of the very few cases of its kind during the decade of the 1990s, which had been characterised by peacekeeping fiascos rather than successes. The most important question that needed to be asked as the world faced the new millennium was whether this was to be a portent of better times to come, or whether it was an aberration in an otherwise negative landscape of violence, inadequate (or no) response, and impotence.

DISCUSSION QUESTIONS

- Is "ethnic cleansing" the same as genocide, or are they actually two separate activities?
- Should the Serbs have been rewarded for "ethnic cleansing" by being allowed to keep the areas they conquered as the price of peace at Dayton, Ohio?
- Could the United Nations have done more to stop the genocide in Rwanda?
- Why do you think the Western nations turned their back on genocide in Rwanda after April 1994?
- Was the NATO intervention in Kosovo in 1999 an admission of a guilty conscience over its failure to stop the killing in Bosnia between 1992 and 1995?
- Why was the intervention in East Timor successful in stopping genocidal violence, while other interventions and military actions elsewhere during the 1990s were not?

7

SOUTH SUDAN AND DARFUR: GENOCIDE AGAIN

INTO THE TWENTY-FIRST CENTURY

In light of the catastrophes of the 1990s, a number of international initiatives seeking to bring about a genocide-free world for the twenty-first century were suggested. While some of these will be discussed in **Chapter 9**, it should be pointed out that all seemed to be thwarted by the outbreak of two further explosions of genocidal violence. Both took place in the African country of Sudan.

SOUTH SUDAN

Sudan, the largest country in Africa until 2011 (when southern Sudan seceded to form its own sovereign state), achieved independence from Britain on January 1, 1956, but democratic stability was difficult to achieve. In a *coup d'état* on May 25, 1969, Colonel Jaafar el-Nimeiry (1930–2009) became President, abolished parliament, and outlawed all political parties. He was to remain in office until 1985, largely as the result of anti-communist military support – which, during the Cold War, placed him in an advantageous position relative to the West.

From 1983 onwards, Sudan experienced civil war, famine, disease, massive destruction, and genocide in its southern regions.

The roots of the conflict are deep, but the antagonism of the Islamic north towards the largely Christian and animist south was reinforced when Nimeiry rescinded a measure of autonomy that dated back to 1972 (Johnson 2003: 59–74). Henceforth, the north would rule by direct control, with the south's legislative chamber stripped of even its most basic powers. Resource management became a wholly northern concern, and, over time, Islamic *sharia* law was introduced throughout the south (Collins 2008).

In May 1983 a southern military (and US-trained) officer, John Garang, was sent to Bor, the capital of Jonglei State in southern Sudan, to quell a mutiny of 500 southern troops resisting orders to be shipped north. Instead of putting down their mutiny, he joined his brother officers Samuel Gai Tut (d. 1984), William Nyuon (d. 1996), and Keribino Kuanyin Bol (1948–99), and from this nucleus formed two organisations: the Sudan People's Liberation Movement (SPLM) and the Sudan People's Liberation Army (SPLA). Garang became the Chairman of SPLM, and commander-in-chief of SPLA. By the end of July 1983 he had persuaded over 3,000 soldiers to defect to the SPLA, as other army garrisons were also at that time engaging in acts of mutiny against the imposition of Islamic *sharia* law by the Muslim-dominated government in Sudan's capital, Khartoum.

The appearance of the SPLM/A initiated civil war in Sudan. As the national government sought to rein in the separatists, southern Sudan was devastated. The resultant death toll of upwards of 2.5 million people placed Sudan near the top of the list of post-1945 death statistics for single-country conflicts (Travis 2010: 437).

By 1986 the SPLA was estimated to have 12,500 armed men, organised into 12 battalions, and equipped with small arms and mortars – much of it from Garang's backers in Libya, Uganda, and Ethiopia. Support grew even further by 1989, when the SPLA's strength had reached anywhere from 20,000 to 30,000. By 1991 it was estimated that this had risen even further, to between 50,000 and 60,000 (Bartrop 2012: 100–101).

In 1989, following a *coup d'état*, a new government was installed in Khartoum under a northern radical Islamiser, Omar Hassan Ahmad al-Bashir (b. 1945). He shared power with the civilian leader of the National Islamic Front, Dr Hasan al-Turabi (b. 1932). Together, they transformed Sudan into an even more fundamentalist

Islamic state, and intensified the war against the south. Garang refused to enter into negotiations as long as this forced attempt to Islamise southern Sudan remained Khartoum's goal, and chose to remain a rebel. While some explanations for the massive number of deaths focus on the destructive nature of the civil war – and it was, certainly, a conflict in which little quarter was given – there is nonetheless enough circumstantial evidence to be able to lay a charge of genocide at the feet of al-Bashir's government. There was, however, little in the way of international attention directed towards the crisis.

Initially, the SPLA relied on support from Ethiopia's dictator Haile Mariam Mengistu (b. 1937), but his fall from office in 1991 led to the loss of this base. Fortune was to favour Garang later, however. The fact that the United States regarded al-Bashir's government as a leading sponsor of international terrorism, in which the master terrorist Osama bin Laden (1957–2011) was alleged to have been given refuge, only served to throw American support behind anyone willing to oppose the government in Khartoum (Petterson 2003).

Despite this, the Government of Sudan (GoS) was also known to have made half-hearted attempts to lure Garang towards a peace settlement – even though he always declined on the basis that to do so would be to leave the south vulnerable to northern economic exploitation, and religious and ethnic persecution.

A painfully slow negotiating process did, however, take place, as both sides accepted that they were deadlocked in a war that neither could win. In July 2002, Garang and al-Bashir met for the first time, in Uganda, and a breakthrough came when the south was granted the right to hold a referendum on its future after a six-year transition period. The SPLM agreed to put its demand for secession on hold, and in return the GoS agreed to a limited separation between the state and religion, and to withdraw most of its troops from the south.

The peace process dragged on for another 18 months, during which haggling took place over how the south's oil revenues were to be split. In May 2004 a provisional peace agreement was signed. This was followed by a Comprehensive Peace Agreement, negotiated at Naivasha, Kenya, and signed on January 9, 2005 between the SPLA and the GoS. It provided for Garang's appointment as

Vice-President of Sudan in a power-sharing arrangement that allowed limited autonomy for southern Sudan and a scheduled referendum on possible secession within six years. On July 9, 2005, after 21 years of struggle, John Garang entered Khartoum to a rapturous welcome, and was sworn in as Vice-President.

Less than three weeks later, in late July 2005, he was returning by helicopter from a visit to Rwakitura, the country home of his long-time ally, Ugandan President Yoweri Museveni (b. 1944). In circumstances the full details of which are still yet to be fully determined, the helicopter crashed, and Garang and all on board were killed. At first, there was uncertainty as to what the effect of Garang's death might be upon the Naivasha Agreement, but the peace held sufficiently to enable a referendum to take place in January 2011 to determine whether the region should remain part of Sudan or become independent. On February 7, 2011, the referendum commission published the final results, with 98.83 per cent voting in favour of independence. Accordingly, on July 9, 2011, the Republic of South Sudan became Africa's newest independent country, and the 193rd member state of the United Nations.

After South Sudan's independence in 2011, the border region known as South Kordofan remained under the control of the GoS. Within the region, fears existed of future communal violence as residents of the Nuba Mountains specifically, and South Kordofan generally, threatened to take up arms so that they could leave Sudan and join the new state to the south. By way of response, the GoS retained a heavy military presence in the region, and reports of indiscriminate bombing of civilians emerged throughout 2012 and 2013. While the international community has again shown interest, little of value has been done to rectify the situation. Once more, al-Bashir's regime has been in the spotlight, and a watching brief on South Kordofan and the Nuba Mountains has been maintained lest these might become a new site of genocide.

DARFUR

Beginning in 2003, al-Bashir's regime engaged in a "scorched earth" campaign against those who describe themselves as the "black Africans" of Darfur. A region roughly the size of France, Darfur is located in the western part of Sudan, bordering Libya,

Chad, and the Central African Republic. Prior to the outbreak of violence in 2003, Darfur had a population consisting of dozens of different tribal groups, of whom a large minority were considered "Arab" and a majority were classed as "non-Arab" or black African. Due to intermarriage, the distinction between the two peoples owes more to lifestyle differences and cultural affiliation than to race. Darfuri Arabs tend to lead nomadic lives, herding cattle and camels throughout the region, while for the most part non-Arabs are sedentary farmers.

For years, the Fur, Masalit, and Zaghawa ethnic groups had been calling on the GoS to use monies from the taxes they paid to help develop their region, especially through the building of roads, schools, and hospitals. They also called for better treatment of black Africans at the hands of the police and judicial system. Further, they complained bitterly that Arabs in the region were given preferential treatment over black Africans.

When they felt their complaints were falling on deaf ears, a rebel group, the Sudanese Liberation Army (SLA), was formed, and in early 2003 it began carrying out attacks against government and military installations. Short-handed due to the much larger and more destructive civil war in southern Sudan, al-Bashir hired nomadic Arabs to join forces with GoS troops to fight the rebels. However, instead of focusing their attacks, the GoS and local militia groups known as *Janjaweed* carried out a scorched earth policy against *all* black Africans in Darfur. The campaign led to the GoS and *Janjaweed* indiscriminately killing men, women, and children, raping young girls and women, and, prior to burning down entire villages, plundering what they could (Reeves 2007).

The term *Janjaweed* is an Arabic composite of *jinn* (spirit or ghost) and *jawad* (horse) that once was used to describe wild outlaws. Colloquially, the name is used to mean "devils (or evil men) on horseback" (or sometimes, depending on the context, camels) (Steidle with Steidle Wallace 2007). From 2003 onwards, *Janjaweed* was the label given to the Arab militiamen who carried out the genocidal attacks along with the GoS troops.

In a classic case of deliberate destruction, the attacks followed a set-pattern formula: a fighter plane would arrive and circle around a village to conduct reconnaissance, followed by helicopter gunships that would hover above the village and shoot at anything that moved. Eyewitness accounts describe how Sudanese government forces and *Janjaweed* would then sweep in on trucks or a combination of horses, camels, and motor vehicles, wielding automatic weapons and firing indiscriminately at civilians. Homes, grain stores, and crops were destroyed, while women, children, and the elderly were whipped, raped, tortured, and, frequently, murdered. The village would then be burned and looted, but not before the *Janjaweed* had taken goods for themselves as payment for their efforts (Steidle with Steidle Wallace 2007). Some of these "villages" were in reality small towns, and their destruction resulted in hundreds of thousands of displaced civilians. These tactics were designed to terrorise the victims, forcing them to flee their homelands. Once gone, Arab populations would resettle the land, effectively eradicating the rebels' power base. By 2006, estimates of those killed ranged upward to 400,000, with well over two million Darfuris internally displaced and another 250,000 in refugee camps in Chad (Mikaberidze 2013: 621).

INTERNATIONAL REACTION

Initial reaction to the conflict in Darfur was inadequate, as bystanders such as the United Nations, the United States, and the European Union chose to prioritise other foreign policy issues over the escalating crisis in Darfur – in particular the invasion, on March 19, 2003, of Iraq by a joint coalition led by the US and Britain. This started without United Nations approval and in defiance of world opinion, and was to dominate international developments for years to come. Many actors in the international community deliberately preferred not to notice what was happening in Darfur in order not to rock the boat.

Al-Bashir and his government continually denied that a campaign of genocide was taking place, and argued that the casualty and death figures were grossly inflated. They rejected accusations that they were supporting aggression by the *Janjaweed* against the black African rebel groups, claiming that foreigners had "fabricated" and "exaggerated" the conflict.

In 2003 a British medical doctor, Mukesh Kapila (b. 1955), was appointed as the United Nations' Resident Humanitarian Coordinator, and UN Development Programme Resident Representative, in Sudan. As such, he became the UN's top official in that country.

He took up his new post just a few months after Darfuri rebels first attacked GoS military outposts. Kapila did not have any international observers in Darfur, so it took some time to fully appreciate that something altogether new and catastrophic was happening. From the middle of 2003, personal accounts began to trickle out with the first displaced people arriving in Khartoum, and local UN personnel were also passing on reports to Kapila's office. As news of atrocities mounted from late 2003 onwards, he began to see a pattern. Reports showed that GoS forces and *Janjaweed* were using scorched-earth tactics against black African Darfuri civilians. Villages were being burned, wells were being poisoned, and women and girls were being raped in large numbers. Kapila was forced to conclude that what was taking place in Darfur was indeed ethnic cleansing; after a while, he arrived at the view that he was in fact witnessing the first genocide of the twenty-first century. His immediate reaction was that he should attempt to develop a deeper understanding of what was going on in Darfur, and he began actively to work to stop the carnage (Kapila 2013).

In early 2004, Kapila informed his superiors at UN headquarters in New York of his conclusions. The response he received was that as Resident Humanitarian Coordinator he should not get involved in political concerns outside his remit. A second response was that the peace process was in the hands of powers other than the United Nations (though with that body's approval), and that little would be achieved by the Department of Political Affairs in New York getting involved.

Kapila was disgusted, but not discouraged. He attempted to raise awareness of the situation, beginning with the government of Sudan itself. He also spoke with members of the international community, starting with the foreign diplomatic corps stationed in Khartoum. From there, he began to make personal visits to governments abroad. He first went to his own government in London, then to Washington, DC (where he had meetings at the National Security Council in the White House), Paris, Oslo, Brussels, Rome, and many other cities. In some countries, his discussions were at ministerial level; in others, with senior bureaucrats. Wherever he went, he was told that the governments in question knew what was happening but that, because of the delicate negotiations then taking place to try to bring the war in southern Sudan to an end, now was not the time to upset the situation by making a fuss over Darfur. Only in Washington did he obtain anything like a full hearing, but, even then, no concrete action was taken. The general attitude seemed to be that a greater provision of humanitarian aid was needed, rather than resolving what were, in reality, political problems requiring immediate resolution.

In frustration, Kapila abandoned the route of normal international diplomacy, and in March 2004 went public. From Nairobi, Kenya, he conducted an interview with BBC Radio comparing the situation in Darfur to the 1994 genocide in Rwanda. His comments succeeded in bringing Darfur to the attention of the world's media for the first time. Newspapers around the world picked up the story, which was immediately met by denunciations from the GoS. His outspokenness landed him in trouble with his employer, the United Nations, such that he was withdrawn by the UN in April 2004 and transferred out of Sudan (Kapila 2013).

Building on Kapila's revelations, however, the US State Department and the US Agency for International Development sponsored its own investigation in July and August 2004. The resulting Atrocities Documentation Project saw 24 investigators from around the world interview over 1,100 black African refugees in some 19 refugee camps along the Chad/Sudan border (Totten and Markusen 2006). Based on the analysis of the data collected, on September 9, 2004 Secretary of State Colin Powell (b. 1937) declared, in a report to the Senate Foreign Relations Committee, that Sudan had committed (and possibly still was committing) genocide against the black Africans. Powell's position was affirmed by President George W. Bush (b. 1946) the same day, and then restated in June 2005.

Powell's announcement was historic in that it was the first time one sovereign nation had formally accused another of genocide. During his testimony, Powell also invoked for the first time ever (by any government) Chapter VIII of the UN Convention on Genocide, calling on the Security Council to take action "for the prevention and suppression of acts of genocide."

In following up on this, the US government referred its findings to the UN Security Council, which, in turn, conducted its own study between December 2004 and January 2005 for the express purpose of ascertaining for itself whether, in fact, genocide had been or was being perpetrated in Darfur. Upon analysis of the data collected by its commission of inquiry, the UN declared that it had found ample evidence of serious crimes against humanity, though it did not find that the GoS and *Janjaweed* had committed genocide. That said, it did not rule out that genocidal acts might have been committed, adding that an analysis of further evidence in the future would resolve that one way or another. Subsequently, the UN referred the matter to the International Criminal Court, which then began its own investigation with an eye toward prosecuting the alleged perpetrators. It, in turn, recommended that the Security Council place 17 individuals from the Sudanese government on targeted sanctions, with five others, including al-Bashir, listed as potential targets.

In July 2008, the Prosecutor of the ICC, Luis Moreno Ocampo (b. 1952), accused al-Bashir of having committed genocide, crimes against humanity, and war crimes in Darfur, and on March 4, 2009 the court issued a warrant for al-Bashir's arrest. On July 12, 2010 he was indicted on three counts of genocide, becoming the first sitting head of state to be charged by the ICC and the first to be incriminated for the crime of genocide. Moreno Ocampo also alleged that al-Bashir bore individual criminal responsibility for the crimes for which he had been charged, arguing that he had been the mastermind of a plan to destroy Darfur's three main ethnic groups.

Many human rights observers welcomed the prospect of the Sudanese leader being brought to justice, but, as Sudan was not a party to the Rome Statute that established the ICC, the likelihood of the GoS cooperating appeared to be extremely remote as long as al-Bashir remained in office. Moreover, he treated the ICC warrant with complete contempt, a situation not helped by the fact that many states persisted in paying him the respect due any other head of state not facing such serious charges. Both the Arab League and the African Union condemned the arrest warrant when it was issued on the grounds of neo-colonialist interference in the affairs of a sovereign state, and several countries ignored their international obligations to arrest him. Among the countries he visited after being indicted were Egypt, Qatar, Chad, Nigeria, Turkey, Denmark, Kenya, Djibouti, and Malawi. On June 27, 2011 he was welcomed to Beijing for meetings with China's leader, Hu Jintao (b. 1942).

A number of organisations and individuals were not prepared to let things rest with the formal UN processes, however. Award-winning American actress Mia Farrow (b. 1945), for example, became involved in a range of activities for Darfur that saw her travel to the region in 2004, 2006, and 2007. On the latter visit, she expressed the depth of her concern by offering to trade her freedom for that of a captured Darfuri rebel leader then being treated in a local UN hospital. She offered her own freedom in exchange for him being allowed to leave Sudan without conditions.

In advance of the 2008 Summer Olympics in Beijing, Farrow, together with anti-genocide activist Eric Reeves (b. 1950) and the Director of Public Programs at Human Rights First, Jill Savitt, created a new organisation, Olympic Dream for Darfur. Through this, a publicity campaign began with the intention of forcing the Chinese government, in view of China's close relationship with the GoS and as a Permanent Member of the UN Security Council, to intervene on behalf of Darfur. The campaign focused world atten-tion on China's support for the GoS, embarrassing China in the lead-up to the Olympics. It organised "alternative" torch relays, boycotts of Chinese products, and visits in order to draw attention to what Olympic Dream termed the "Genocide Olympics." By April 2007 it seemed as though Farrow's work was beginning to yield results, as the Beijing government reversed its stance on Darfur and urged Sudan to accept United Nations peacekeepers in the region.

Another of Farrow's signal achievements was in persuading Hollywood's premier movie director, Steven Spielberg (b. 1946) – who had been appointed as artistic adviser for the Opening Ceremony – to withdraw from his position on February 12, 2008. In resigning, he wrote a letter to the Chinese government in which he also urged its leaders to take action over Darfur.

Farrow's detractors argued that she was wrong in singling out China, as the Chinese government was neither committing genocide in Darfur, nor bankrolling the GoS. All the Chinese were guilty of, in this assessment, was seeking to make money out of commercial deals to buy Sudanese oil. In condemning China, Farrow's critics contended, she was, in reality, barking up the wrong tree; China was being targeted only for having commercial relations with Sudan – for which many other Western countries, the United States included, were *not* being demonised.

In April 2011, al-Bashir admitted for the first time that he accepted full personal responsibility for the conflict in Darfur, but accused the ICC of double standards and of conducting a campaign of lies against both himself and Sudan. He accused the West of having imposed on Sudan colonial structures that had caused the conflict in Darfur, but admitted command responsibility as head of state for not having defeated the insurgents of the SLA.

In December 2010, representatives of the Liberation and Justice Movement, an umbrella organisation of ten rebel groups, started negotiations with the GoS in Doha, Qatar. These talks ended without a peace agreement but with a set of basic principles in place, including the possible establishment of a regional authority and a referendum on autonomy for Darfur. Then, throughout 2011, there were a number of additional proposals and counter-proposals, rejections and acceptances of specific points, and continued back-channel dialogue. As of the time of writing, negotiations are continuing, though much of the organised killing has come to an end for the time being. That said, the situation remains volatile, with significant inter-communal violence and fighting between GoS forces and rebels. In late 2013, the UN reported that over 460,000 people had been displaced in Darfur during the year, more than the number in 2011 and 2012 combined (http://www.securitycouncilreport.org/monthly-forecast/2014-01/sudan_darfur_3.php).

ASSESSING DARFUR

The catastrophe in Darfur represents, arguably, the first genocide of the twenty-first century. Estimates of the number of dead have ranged from 250,000 to over 400,000 (Mikaberidze 2013: 621), in what Roméo Dallaire, the former head of UNAMIR at the time of the Rwandan Genocide of 1994, has described as "Rwanda in slow motion" (Pigott 2009: 170). Despite the failures of the international community during the 1990s, little was done to prevent the massive death rate that took place in the eyes of the world's media and political leaders after 2003. It is unclear whether or not the international mismanagement of the Darfur crisis is likely to act as a precedent for similar genocidal situations in the future, but the prognosis for Sudan is not good.

While hopes exist that the tragedy of Darfur might serve as a sufficient shock to the international system that the promise of "never again" might yet be realised, it is clear that there is still a very long way to go if the twenty-first century is not to be a continuation of the twentieth century, which was "the century of genocide."

DISCUSSION QUESTIONS

- Does the conflict in Darfur provide a just reason for international intervention?
- Should the resolution of the conflict in Darfur be an African responsibility alone?
- In your view, was there a war of genocidal destruction waged in Darfur? If so, why?
- Was the international response to the Darfur crisis after 2003 adequate, and how can this be measured?

OTHER CASES: PROBLEMS OF CLASSIFICATION

APPLYING THE TERM

Despite nearly seven decades of discussion and application, genocide is a term that is still misunderstood and often misapplied. Ever since it was first coined there have been disputes about how it should be defined and interpreted (Shaw 2007; Totten and Bartrop 2008: 101–102, 162). Not only have these been vigorous and, at times, acrimonious, they have also often led to substantial and significant misuse.

As a result, genocide has sometimes been equated directly with war, with language extinction, or with massive population losses caused through famine or disease. The term genocide can also be misapplied when conflated into other examples of inhumanity or gross human rights violation, such as, for example, slavery. The popularisation and misuse of the term has been especially pronounced in the realms of education and journalism, where anyone's definition or understanding of the term is seemingly just as legitimate as anyone else's.

Yet only a few of the many tragedies confronting humanity, breath-taking in the scale of the suffering they inflict on millions of people though they are, can ever be accepted as genocide legally. The primary condition needed to bring a successful prosecution – a demonstrable intention to destroy a group – often simply does not exist. Departing from the universally recognised appreciation of genocide, as embodied in the United Nations Convention on Genocide, leads to conceptual confusion in an area requiring clarity and precision, and it is this kind of misunderstanding that must be avoided. Conceptual accuracy is critical when identifying a situation as being or not being genocide.

The UN Convention on Genocide embraces more than just killing, even though, for many, this is the most apparent manifestation of what genocide is all about. Nor, however, does it cover everything, even though, perhaps, we would often prefer that it did. This is why we must be careful – indeed, respectful – when invoking it.

In this chapter, consideration will be given to some of the "difficult" areas in which discussion of genocide takes place. Several will be considered, following which a number of further case studies – not, perhaps, as clear-cut as those already explored – will be examined.

CULTURAL GENOCIDE

The notion of "cultural genocide" is frequently employed when meaning the deliberate destruction of a group's culture and its enforced replacement by another. It is a broad term that unavoidably overlaps other explanations for genocide. Even though the UN Convention on Genocide does not explicitly recognise a category of "cultural genocide" – thus rendering the term irrelevant in international law – cultural destruction can certainly take place that contributes to genocide as measured by other criteria.

The term culture, broadly speaking, embraces such factors as language and literature, art, artefacts, and architectural monuments, as well as a common past; in short, all the ingredients that help a group to forge a collective identity. Were a group's cultural heritage to be systematically destroyed, in whole or in part, its group identity would certainly be weakened: thus, as an example, the destruction of archives, libraries, and art galleries could seriously undermine the sense of a group's past. Similarly, loss of language could endanger a group's collective future. The targeting of ancient churches and libraries could easily weaken group morale and cause other psychological damage. Illustrations are many and diverse: the Nazis in Germany burning books by Jews in 1933 and synagogues in 1938; Stalin forbidding the use of the Ukrainian and Yiddish languages, and generally stamping out religious life throughout the USSR; the Khmer Rouge's utter obliteration of Cambodia's colonial past, together with all schools, temples, and religious practice; and Bosnian Serbs consciously shelling the historic library of Sarajevo, destroying its precious collection of books and ancient manuscripts.

It must be borne in mind, however, that cultural destruction does not always equate with genocide, and that there is no official category that can specifically be termed "cultural genocide."

WAR AND GENOCIDE

Sometimes, war and genocide are equated as synonymous. In the popular consciousness, the first thing that can come to mind is the idea of killing on a vast scale. Genocide is almost always seen as having something to do with death – brutal death, massive of type, and uncompromising in its choice of victim. And more often than not, armies in war are seen as the major vehicles by which this killing takes place. There can be little doubt that war contains within it the potential for a genocidal regime to realise its aims, and probably more easily than in peacetime. Yet war does not have to be present for genocide to occur; genocide does not equate with war, and the two terms should not be employed interchangeably (Bartrop 2002).

Traditionally, the concept of war involves the killing of large numbers of people, specifically soldiers in combat. War can create a variety of dispositions leading to genocide, whereby massive human destruction is facilitated through such features as depersonalisation, social violence, extensions of government power, and alienation of victim groups.

As the key to understanding whether an incident may or may not be described as genocide, the question of *intent* is crucial. Clearly, there are some cases in the history of warfare when the intent to destroy entire groups is both obvious and declared by a perpetrator, either in advance or during the destruction itself. But war, on its own, need not be synonymous with genocide, in view of the fact that there are occasions on which neither the intent nor a declaration of intent would appear to exist.

The destructive character of the last century cannot be ignored, but genocide has rarely been a mere by-product of conflict. Instead, it has stemmed from a long-standing obsession on the part of the perpetrators with the physical, political, social, psychological, religious, or cultural differences of the victim group – differences so great and irreconcilable that the perpetrators could see no solution to the situation except elimination of "the other" through mass annihilation.

In the modern era, the concept of Total War has come to mean the waging of war on a civilian population, bombing of cities, causing famine by blockading food supplies, and the like (Slim 2007; Markusen and Kopf 1995). It has also meant using all means possible to destroy an enemy. There are certainly areas where war crosses over into genocide. Sometimes, compromise is impossible in the quest for total victory, leading to the most radical means of destruction.

An example is Italian dictator Benito Mussolini's (1883–1945) colonial war against the Empire of Abyssinia in 1935. Despite the enemy's obvious military weakness, fascist Italy employed poison gas against civilian villages, resulting in the most horrible deaths and a huge loss of life (Duggan 2013; Gooch 2007: 252–314). The same phenomenon can be found in Saddam Hussein's indiscriminate use of lethal gas in his war with Iran, and in his internal wars against the Kurdish and Shi'ite minorities in Iraq (Hiltermann 2007). Sufficient examples abound to demonstrate the interconnection between Total War and outright genocide. One could almost argue that the military totalistic mentality is a *sine qua non* for genocide.

It is here that the issue is at its most contentious. War, generally speaking, creates a number of conditions (psychological, social, and political) favourable to the prospect of genocidal killing. Some have taken this further, arguing that strategic bombing in wartime, such as at Hamburg, Dresden, Tokyo, Hiroshima, and Nagasaki, is itself genocidal (Markusen and Kopf 1995). Seen from this perspective, war – or at least a certain dimension of it – is a genocidal force in and of itself. In this context, we can be looking at war *as* genocide rather than war *in* genocide.

FAMINE

When a population faces a period of extreme scarcity of food, resulting in widespread starvation and death, it can be said to be experiencing famine. Throughout history, famines have occurred mostly as a result of natural disasters. Sometimes, governments have been able to foresee scarcity and plan for its eventuality in advance, stockpiling food reserves and riding out the worst until circumstances improved. More frequently, however, societies have experienced devastating periods of mass starvation, possibly accompanied by pestilence and disease, and often resulting in population collapses.

Just as in nature, famine can also occur with catastrophic results when deliberately planned and executed by a government over part of its own population, or over the population of a country with which it is at war. Examples abound, from the salting of arable land by the Romans at Carthage after 146 BCE, the killing of buffalo herds in the Great Plains of the United States in the nineteenth century, and the killing off of crops through the use of defoliants in Vietnam and Biafra in the 1960s.

In other instances, perpetrators have destroyed populations more deliberately through the withholding of food or changing the means of its distribution, such that a victim population is deprived of sustenance it normally would have counted on for survival.

In Ireland, the period known as the Great Hunger (*an Gorta Mór*) saw mass starvation, disease, and emigration between 1845 and 1852. It is sometimes referred to, mostly outside Ireland, as the Irish Potato Famine. The famine is a controversial event in Irish history, and rests on the level of complicity of the United Kingdom in providing appropriate assistance to the Irish after the potato crop, on which a third of the population depended for its survival, failed. Several historians have argued that British complacency sought deliberately to reduce the Irish population (Coogan 2012); others have argued that while British actions appear to be genocide, there were various factors that do not permit such a conclusion (Ó Gráda 2000). Elsewhere, commentators have argued that the memory of the famine has had a similar effect on Irish culture as would be expected of a population that had experienced genocide (Woodham-Smith 1962).

The key issue to be decided in cases such as these is how far the perpetrator's intention is to use famine for the purpose of destroying the victim population, or how far its intention is to destroy the victim population's will to resist, or to force resettlement, or to otherwise bring about an alteration in the behaviour of the victim group. Some instances are clear-cut. In Ukraine between 1932 and 1933, the twin Soviet aims of destroying Ukrainian national identity and redistributing Ukrainian food from the country to the cities to feed communist industrialisation had a devastating effect, resulting in the deliberate death of at least seven million people (Conquest 1986; Davies and Wheatcroft 2004). As another example, the intention of the Nazis in reducing the daily rations of Jews in the ghettos during the Holocaust was that they would die of starvation.

Intent is thus the most vital determinant of whether a famine situation is or is not genocidal, the more so as regimes have throughout history also taken advantage of food shortages in order to "solve" domestic problems involving unwanted populations. Thus, while famine can be an unfortunate result of an act of nature, it can also be deliberately conceived and executed, either to destroy a population or (more commonly) to address an issue. In assessing famine and genocide, every instance must be measured on a case-by-case basis.

SLAVERY

A slave is a person who is the legal property of another party, in which the relationship is unequal and established on a principle of total obedience to total authority. Slavery almost always implies severe manual labour, for little or no reward on the part of the slave. It has a history dating back to ancient times, and slaves have routinely been taken as a spoil of war. Sometimes, men would be separated from women after the conquest of a city or territory, and both sexes would be sent as slaves to separate destinations. While this could have had the effect of destroying the basis of a group's identity, the reasons behind such separation and slavery were less likely for ideology than for pragmatic reasons, such as a need for labour or to generate wealth through selling the slaves as property.

In such situations, where both the ownership of slaves and the slave system itself requires that slaves stay alive, a genocidal impulse is usually suppressed on the part of the slave owners in favour of profit maximisation. This should not suggest, however, that the operation of slave societies passed without brutality and death (to say nothing of a massive violation of human rights). Indeed, the initial capturing of slaves has almost always been accompanied by killing and death (sometimes, as on the Middle Passage between Africa and the Americas, on an enormous scale). Indeed, it is usually only those who survive this phase of capture and transportation who are transformed into slaves. And sometimes, it must be pointed out, this is a minority of those who are initially captured. In the twentieth century, slavery took on a new guise, within an overall global environment, as brutal regimes transformed local occupied populations (such as the Congolese at the hands of the Belgians), or minority populations (such as Jews under Hitler's Nazis), or dominant populations (such as the Cambodians under Pol Pot's Khmer Rouge) into slave communities (Fein 2007).

For all that, it is important to bear in mind that slavery does not equate with genocide. Despite the huge number of deaths it can generate, slavery by definition does not specifically seek the destruction of a specific group or groups, but, rather, their preservation for the purpose of continued exploitation.

CHALLENGING CASE STUDIES

Any study of genocide must consider the existence of cases of mass destruction that, for one reason or another, are difficult to classify. It does not in the slightest alter the horror, the deaths, or the pain the survivors feel at what has happened (or the repulsion that we, who were not directly involved, should feel), but it does require us to look into the nature of the destruction in order to explain it and assign responsibility where it is appropriate. A sampling of such cases helps to illustrate this.

BIAFRA

The Igbo are a large ethnic group concentrated in south-east Nigeria, who can trace their presence in the region back to the ninth century CE. After Nigeria's independence from British colonial rule in 1960, thousands of Igbo migrated to the Muslim-dominated north of the country in search of work, where they lived in communities that were strictly segregated from the Muslim majority.

In early 1966, the Igbo were held responsible – falsely – by the Federal Government of Nigeria, led by military dictator General Yakubu Gowon (b. 1934), for the murder of several military officials, resulting in murderous riots. Violence escalated throughout the year and Igbo deaths rose from hundreds to thousands, provoking their wholesale flight from the north back to their traditional home in the south-east. This, in turn, led to calls for an Igbo secession movement, in large measure because the central government seemed unable to curb anti-Igbo violence (Gould 2012: 33–38).

Encouraging the Igbo in their belief that a viable breakaway state could be established was the knowledge that large reserves of high-grade oil lay beneath the Igbo heartland. In May 1967 the Eastern State seceded, and, under the leadership of Lieutenant-Colonel (Emeka) Chukwuemeka Odumegwu Ojukwu (1933–2011), created an Igbo majority state called Biafra (Forsyth 1977: 81–107).

The Nigerian army invaded immediately, with the intention of dragging Biafra back into the Federation. The war that ensued, from the summer of 1967 onward, escalated rapidly. One of the weapons employed by the government of Nigeria – acknowledged openly by ministers and military figures alike – was to cut off food supplies to the civilian population. Igbo leaders, both in Biafra and abroad, labelled this as genocide, and appeals were made to the UN to recognise Biafra and to intervene in order to save the population. It was the first time the charge of genocide was made in the international environment since the term was codified in 1948. The UN turned down the Igbo request to be heard, however, on the ground that UN membership was limited to recognised states only, a status Biafra had not yet received. The Nigeria–Biafra War was therefore considered to be a domestic matter, and thus outside the scope of the UN (Stremlau 1977).

The war, which lasted from June 1967 until January 1970, took a terrible toll on the Igbo. It resulted in the death of up to a million people (Totten and Bartrop 2008: 205–206) including an estimated 500,000 children between the ages of one and 10 years (Forsyth 1977: 257), and the effects did not end with the military collapse. Civilian infrastructure – roads, bridges, schools, hospitals, towns, buildings of all kinds, homes – had been utterly destroyed. Large numbers of the Igbo intellectual and economic elite left in fear of their lives, forming a dispersed community in Europe, North America, and other African countries.

To what degree can we call the fate of the Igbo people, and the inhabitants of Biafra, genocide? The answer, at first, would seem to be clear-cut. Massive physical destruction was accompanied by population displacement and deliberately imposed policies of starvation, in which a huge civilian death toll was recorded (Ezeh 2012).

The Nigeria–Biafra War was the first occasion in which scenes of mass starvation were brought home to a television-dominated West, and millions throughout Europe, North America, and elsewhere were horrified by what they saw. Less apparent was the reality that lay behind this otherwise simple case of a brutal and bloody secessionist conflict, for, in Nigeria's determination to defeat the Biafran breakaway state, the Nigerians engineered conditions of famine, and the Nigerian air force carpet-bombed Igbo population centres (especially refugee establishments, churches, schools, hospitals, markets, homes, farmlands, and playgrounds). Nigerian officials held mass starvation to be a legitimate aspect of war, clearly expressing what might be held as an intention to destroy Biafra's attempt at secession through the destruction of the population's will to resist (Gould, 2012).

But was it genocide, a deliberate attempt to destroy the Biafran population – and in particular the Igbo – *as a group*? A deliberately designed policy of enforced famine was perpetrated, but was the result a case of a genocidal outcome, though without a genocidal design? In which case, can it be called a policy of genocide? The question, though arising from time to time in academic discourse, has never been officially discussed in any formal decision-making forum.

CHINA AND TIBET

China has experienced significant episodes of genocidal destruction over the past century. It would be a mistake to think that its people have only suffered under communism, even though the killing has predominated over the course of communist rule since 1949. Under the rule of warlords and the pre-1949 Nationalist government, millions were killed – deliberately, for political reasons, and as innocent victims swept up in the course of the many wars and rebellions that beset China during the first half of the twentieth century (Rummel 1991).

These atrocities were not only caused through internal upheaval, however: China's experience at the hands of its Japanese occupiers throughout the 1930s led to a low estimate of four million deaths, possibly up to six million (Rummel 1991). Over a six-week period starting on December 17, 1937, China's then capital city, Nanking (Nanjing), became a paradigm for genocidal massacre as the Japanese, in an orgy of murder, rape, torture, and looting, killed more than 300,000 of the city's residents (Chang 1997).

After the communist victory in October, 1949 following a brutal civil war with the Nationalists, millions of Chinese citizens were killed as the party sought to develop its revolutionary platform and shape society according to the teachings of the party chairman, Mao Zedong (1893–1976). The communists employed ferocious repression in order to terrorise the population into following the new ways. They executed all those who had represented the former Nationalist government or its ideals; those whom the communists deemed to be counter-revolutionaries; and anyone else considered an "enemy" of the people (Rummel 1991). Perhaps up to 30 million more lost their lives owing to starvation and more political killing in the communist drive to institutionalise the revolution through schemes of social engineering, such as the Great Leap Forward (1958–62) and the Cultural Revolution (1966–76) (Margolin 1999).

Under communism, China has had a record of unrelenting state-imposed death on a genocidal scale, and to this should be added a clear-cut case of genocide against the people of Tibet, invaded by China in 1950. Since then, there has been an ongoing and intensive campaign of cultural destruction carried out by successive Chinese governments against the Tibetans (Levenson 2011: 91–105).

The Chinese position since the invasion has been that it was for the good of those living there under the feudal monastic rule of the 14th Dalai Lama (Tenzin Gyatso, b. 1935; reigned 1950 to the present). In the decades following the invasion, the people of Tibet and their Buddhist way of life were subjected to immense devastation. It has been estimated that at least two million Tibetans died as a result of the ongoing Chinese incursion, a result of military conflict, famine, or harsh captivity in prison camps (Totten and Bartrop 2008: 421).

While Chinese occupation has undoubtedly been murderous on an immense scale, the question of genocide is problematical within the meaning of the UN Convention on Genocide due to the absence of a perceived intent to destroy the Tibetans as an identifiable group. It is thus a challenge to draw a definite conclusion that the communist regime, while guilty of many other crimes, is also culpable specifically of the crime of genocide, despite it being one of the regimes least concerned with the preservation of human life during its attempts to reconstruct society in accordance with its ambitions.

SIERRA LEONE AND LIBERIA

Between 1991 and 2002 an 11-year-long terror campaign and civil war was launched against the west African country of Sierra Leone from neighbouring Liberia. At least 50,000 people died (Bartrop 2012: 313). At its heart was the group responsible for the violence, the Revolutionary United Front (RUF), and its leader, Foday Sankoh (1937–2003).

A soldier by profession, Sankoh had received military training in Libya under its dictator, Muammar Gaddafi (1942–2011). It was here that Sankoh met a young Liberian, Charles Taylor (b. 1948), also undergoing training. Sankoh and Taylor would become comrades-in-arms in West Africa, eventually laying waste to both their countries. After Libya, Sankoh moved to Liberia, where, in 1988–9, he and others formed the RUF. With the help of Taylor and others he recruited local youths and launched his terror campaign.

The insurrection began as an idealistic movement to rid Sierra Leone of the corrupt government of Major-General Joseph Saidu Momoh (1937–2003). The endeavour quickly degenerated, however, into a movement in which out-of-control thugs pillaged the countryside, raping, looting, and enriching themselves on the bodies of their own people. The RUF's first assault took place on March 23, 1991.

At first, the RUF attracted some measure of support from the rural poor, as Sankoh promised to introduce free health care and education, and a fair distribution of natural diamond revenues. But having captured the diamond fields, he used the profits to buy arms from Taylor, the better to be able to extend his rapacious activities. Instead of paying his soldiers, he preferred that they would make ends meet by looting the villages they occupied. Moreover, a great many of his troops were children who had been kidnapped, drugged, and forced to commit atrocities, frequently against their own families, as their introduction to life in the RUF (Beah 2008).

Sankoh's army became notorious as a brutal group of rebels whose fighters used machetes to hack off the hands, feet, lips, and ears of Sierra Leone's civilians, and raped thousands of girls and women. Much of the violence was motivated by Sankoh's determination to ensure that local people would not be able to cultivate their crops in order to provide food for the government. His violence was also employed as a disincentive for people to vote in elections (Bartrop 2012: 290–292).

By the end of the 1990s, the conflict had left Sierra Leone in a disastrous condition, and the UN at one point considered the country to be the world's poorest nation. It was unclear what the RUF actually stood for, but few were taken in for long by Sankoh's earlier proclamations opposing government corruption or the introduction of a better regime for Sierra Leone.

The international community, in particular the United Kingdom and the Economic Community of West African States Monitoring Group, or ECOMOG, eventually took a stand, forcing the RUF and the government to come to the negotiating table. In Lomé, the capital of Togo, a peace agreement was signed on July 7, 1999 between Sankoh and the President of Sierra Leone, Ahmad Tejan Kabbah (b. 1932). The deal gave Sankoh a number of cabinet posts in a new government, and a general amnesty for the RUF was decreed. When war threatened once more and the settlement seemed in danger of breaking down, Britain and ECOMOG sent an intervention force into Sierra Leone to impose peace and bring the RUF's brutality to an end. On January 18, 2002, the war officially ended. The government, supported by a large UN peacekeeping force, re-imposed its authority over the country, and the RUF's disarmament and demobilisation took place successfully.

On May 17, 2000, Sankoh was captured. He was indicted by a UN-supported international tribunal, the Special Court for Sierra

Leone (SCSL), charged with 17 counts of war crimes and crimes against humanity that included the use of child soldiers, rape, sexual slavery, enslavement, and extermination. On July 29, 2003, he died in custody in a Freetown hospital after complications set in following a stroke.

In Liberia, Charles Taylor saw Sankoh's incursion into Sierra Leone as an opportunity for his own personal advancement, and in 1991 he took the opportunity to invade Sierra Leone, too. This saw Taylor accused of war crimes and crimes against humanity, as he backed the RUF by assisting them through the sale of weapons in exchange for so-called "blood diamonds" – that is, diamonds mined in a war zone and sold to finance an insurgency (Campbell 2004). It was further alleged that he aided and abetted RUF atrocities against civilians that left many thousands abducted, tortured, mutilated, or killed, while he was also accused of forcibly recruiting child soldiers.

These developments occurred at the same time as Taylor was conducting two civil wars of his own in Liberia, cementing himself in power. Establishing the National Patriotic Front of Liberia, in December 1989 his forces overthrew the government of President Samuel Doe (1951–90). Civil war broke out, however, when one of his commanders, Prince Johnson (b. 1952), broke away and formed his own group, the Independent National Patriotic Front of Liberia. In September 1990, Johnson captured Monrovia, depriving Taylor of outright victory and causing the near-complete breakdown of authority across the country. The civil war became a bloody ethnic conflict, with seven different warlords fighting for control of the country (Gberie 2005).

On March 29, 2006, Taylor was arrested and transferred to Freetown, where he was delivered to the Special Court for Sierra Leone. On June 20, 2006, he was sent on to the tribunal in The Hague (see **Chapter 10**). His trial began on June 4, 2007, and the verdict was announced on April 26, 2012. He was found guilty on all 11 counts of "aiding and abetting" war crimes and crimes against humanity, specifically acts of terrorism, murder, violence against life, health and physical or mental well-being through murder, rape, sexual slavery and other forms of sexual violence, outrages upon personal dignity, cruel treatment, other inhumane acts, conscripting or enlisting children under the age of 15 years into armed forces or groups, or using them to participate actively in hostilities, enslavement, and pillage. For his crimes, Taylor was sentenced to 50 years in prison.

UGANDA

Joseph Kony (b. 1961) is the head of a violent guerrilla movement operating from northern Uganda, known as the Lord's Resistance Army (LRA). The fundamental ambition of the LRA is to establish a new form of government in Uganda, based on the Christian Bible and the Ten Commandments.

It is believed that Kony was born into the Acholi tribe in 1961. As a teenager he became an apprentice witch doctor under his older brother, and it is likely that many of his later mystical and occultist views were formed at this time. He graduated to full witch doctor status when his brother died. He did not complete his high school education, though he is remembered by those who knew him as an amiable boy who played football and was an excellent dancer in the traditional Acholi Larakaraka dance style.

In January 1986, a takeover of power in Uganda occurred at the hands of Yoweri Museveni (b. 1944). Those ranged against him were mostly Acholi or Langi, supporters of President Tito Lutwa Okello (1914–96), himself an Acholi. Museveni and his National Resistance Army (NRA) were perceived as wanting to take power from the Acholi people. As Museveni's NRA marched victoriously into the capital, Kampala, Okello's followers fled north, into southern Sudan. Fear of retribution spread quickly among the Acholis who had fought against the NRA, and, as they regrouped to form the Uganda People's Army, Kony provided them with his spiritual guidance and blessing.

Kony's own rebel group went through several manifestations and names over many years: the Lord's Army (1987–8), the Uganda Peoples' Democratic Christian Army (1988–92), and, finally, the Lord's Resistance Army (LRA) in 1992.

Since first beginning operations in 1986, Kony's actions have been the cause of countless expressions of grief and sorrow in Uganda, southern Sudan, the Democratic Republic of Congo (DRC), and the Central African Republic. Large areas of northern Uganda have been held hostage for over two decades through Kony's campaigns of terror, with over two million people displaced and scores of thousands of children captured to serve in his army or as sex slaves (Eichstaedt 2009). Kony's troops have burned entire villages, settlements, and even refugee camps. The LRA has become a byword for killing, raping, kidnapping, and terror. It is renowned for the mutilation of living people, for cutting off lips, ears, fingers, hands, and feet to keep populations in dread (Bartrop 2012: 171–174). Ex-LRA abductees speak of being forced to kill and maim family, friends, and neighbours, as well as participating in grotesque rites such as drinking their victims' blood. In the LRA's wake, starvation has long gripped large parts of northern Uganda, and the fighting has claimed tens of thousands of lives.

While it is not entirely clear what Kony is fighting for, most commentators consider the LRA as primarily a form of quasi-Christian militia that periodically also toys with Acholi nationalism. Whenever former LRA soldiers have spoken about goals or ideals, the usual response has been that Uganda should be ruled according to the Biblical Ten Commandments, held to be some sort of "constitution" for the people of the world to follow. Kony, a self-styled mystic and religious prophet, claims to be waging war on God's direct orders to replace the "ungodly" Ugandan government (Allen and Vlassenroot 2010).

The vast majority of Kony's soldiers have always been children. It is estimated that he has abducted well over 100,000 boys and girls since the LRA started fighting. He has personally taken girls and young women, called them his wives, beaten them into submission, and then raped and impregnated them. At any one time it is estimated that he might have as many as 60 "wives," and he is believed to have fathered up to 100 children (Bartrop 2012: 172–173).

On July 8 and September 27, 2005, the International Criminal Court (ICC) at The Hague issued arrest warrants against Kony and four other LRA leaders. In what were among the earliest warrants issued by the ICC, they were charged with crimes against humanity and war crimes, including murder, rape, sexual slavery, and enlisting children as combatants. Then, on October 13, 2005, ICC Chief Prosecutor Luis Moreno Ocampo released the details of Kony's indictment. Overall, there were 33 charges. Twelve counts involved crimes against humanity, including murder, enslavement, sexual enslavement, and rape. The remaining 21 counts dealt with war crimes, including murder, cruel treatment of civilians, attacking civilian populations, pillage, inducing rape, and forced conscription of children into the rebels. The indictments were met with mixed feelings in Uganda. Some who know Kony argue that he will never surrender or come to a peace settlement because of the ICC warrants.

In the aftermath of the September 11 attacks on the United States, the US declared Kony a terrorist and the LRA a terrorist group. On August 28, 2008, the US Treasury Department placed Kony on its list of "Specially Designated Global Terrorists," a term that carries financial and other penalties. Then, on May 24, 2010, US President Barack Obama (b. 1961) signed into law the Lord's Resistance Army Disarmament and Northern Uganda Recovery Act, making it US policy to protect civilians from the LRA, to apprehend or remove Kony and his top commanders from the battlefield, and to disarm and demobilise whatever remained of the LRA after that. On October 14, 2011, Obama ordered the deployment of a small detachment of 100 combat troops to Uganda to assist the government in tracking Kony down. As of this writing, Kony has not yet been apprehended, and there is little sign that in the near future this situation is likely to change.

THE SOVIET UNION

In the Soviet Union, the communist regime of Josef Stalin recognised early that a distinctive sense of nationhood was a factor militating against the creation of a truly proletarian state. In the multiethnic Soviet Union, the existence of so many separate nationalities posed a threat that Stalin could not ignore, and, as a way to constrain their aspirations, his government introduced measures to exile entire national groups to the interior of the USSR. Deported to places vast distances from their historic homelands, disoriented and removed from familiar networks, the intention was that they would more readily embrace the communist way of life rather than one in which their separate national identities could take hold (Conquest 1970).

Accordingly, in 1937 Soviet Koreans were removed from the Far East to Kazakhstan and Uzbekistan; in 1941 and 1942 the Volga Germans and other *Volksdeutsche* (German communities living outside Germany proper) were rounded up and sent to Kazakhstan and Siberia; in May 1942 Greeks living in the Crimea were deported to Uzbekistan; in late 1943 the Karachays and Kalmyks were sent to Siberia, Kazakhstan, and Kirghizia; and, at various times in 1944, the Chechens and Ingush, Balkars, Crimean Tartars, Meskhetian Turks, Kurds, and Khemshils were deported to Kurdistan, Siberia, and Uzbekistan (Pohl 1999; Conquest 1970).

All in all, between 1937 and 1944 it is estimated that some two million people from 14 distinct nationalities were deported. During and after the deportations, the conditions were so bad that over 400,000 people (and probably more) lost their lives, in some cases cutting deeply into the population size of the smaller nations (Rummel 1990). According to the UN Convention on Genocide, an argument can be put that the deportations were genocide, in that the Soviet government inflicted conditions of life that were intended (where possible) to bring about their physical destruction in whole or in part – through harsh treatment occasioning murder, privation, disease, hunger, social dislocation, and exposure to the elements. In this case, the physical annihilation of individuals within the national groups was not Stalin's intention; rather it was the destruction of the nationalities themselves that was his goal (Naimark 2010; Rummel 1990).

It was only in the late 1980s and the 1990s, with the downfall of communism, that the process began of repatriating many of the survivors and subsequent generations back to their original homelands.

DEMOCRATIC REPUBLIC OF THE CONGO

One of the locations of greatest slaughter in the early twenty-first century has been the Democratic Republic of the Congo (DRC), formerly Zaïre. It has been estimated that civil wars since 1996 have claimed an estimated 5.5 million lives, making it the world's deadliest conflict since the Second World War (Prunier 2008b). Wars raged between 1996 and 1998, and again since 1998; overall, the extremely complicated situation of the conflicts in the DRC has seen the involvement of armed forces from at least seven countries, as well as the intervention of multiple local militias.

When the genocide in neighbouring Rwanda ended in 1994, Hutu perpetrators fled into the eastern provinces of the DRC, where they formed the *Forces Démocratiques de Libération du Rwanda* (FDLR). The presence of these *génocidaires* prompted an invasion by Rwanda and Uganda, which in turn led to the overthrow of Zaïrean dictator Mobutu Sese Seko (1930–97). Laurent Désiré Kabila (1939–2001), who led the rebellion to overthrow Mobutu, became President. He then declared war on his former allies, Rwanda and Uganda.

As a direct result, ethnic hostility, much of it echoing from the Rwandan genocide and fed by inter-group violence, has produced an environment where groups fear their entire existence is under threat. This has led to catastrophic results for the civilian population. Violence takes many forms, including mass killings, rape, and torture. While this has been an important factor in the huge mortality rate, most have died from disease, starvation, and the effects of social dislocation (Stearns 2011).

In the eastern part of the country, the war never conclusively ended. A range of armed forces, including the *Forces Armées de la République Démocratique du Congo* (Armed Forces of the Democratic Republic of Congo, or FARDC), continue to perpetrate violence against the civilian population. This includes displacement, abductions, looting, forceful recruitment and use of child soldiers, and massive sexual violence.

In 1999 the United Nations authorised the creation of a mission to the DRC, to be known by its acronym, MONUC (*Mission des Nations Unies en République démocratique du Congo*, or United Nations Organisation Mission in the Democratic Republic of the Congo). Its task was to plan for the observation of UN-brokered ceasefire agreements and the subsequent disengagement of forces. It would also maintain liaison with all the parties involved. MONUC was mandated by three UN Security Council resolutions to cooperate with the Congolese government in assisting the process that would lead to suspected war criminals being brought to justice.

The deadly morass in the DRC, dubbed by some as "Africa's World War," is nothing if not confusing (Prunier 2008b). While the death toll has been massive, the ongoing crisis has generated little in the way of widespread external response. Sadly, the nations of the world – and even more, the world's media – see only the tip of a very large iceberg, if they care to see anything at all.

IRAQ

On August 2, 1990, Iraqi forces invaded neighbouring Kuwait, defeating and occupying the small emirate in the space of two days. Four days later, on August 6, 1990, the UN Security Council imposed sanctions against Iraq, the purpose of which was multi-layered: to compel Iraq to withdraw from Kuwait; to pay reparations; and to disclose and eliminate any weapons of mass destruction in Iraq's possession. The sanctions were to remain in force until May 2003, and banned all trade and financial resources except for certain categories of food and medicine.

The effects of the sanctions on the Iraqi people were manifold, with reports over the next few years of high rates of malnutrition, the absence of medical supplies, and diseases from a lack of clean water. In May 2000 a United Nations Children's Fund (UNICEF) survey noted that almost half the children under 5 years of age suffered from diarrhoea. Literacy dropped as children were held back from school. The country was beset by power shortages and, owing to a lack of spare parts, an inability to repair infrastructure when breakdowns occurred (http://www.unicef.org/evaldatabase/index_29697.html).

It is difficult to measure how many preventable deaths occurred as a result of the UN sanctions after 1990. There is no doubt that the sanctions had an enormously detrimental effect on the Iraqi people, but the degree to which it can be described as genocide, as some who were opposed to the war in Iraq have done, is highly debatable. Any claims that UN actions equated to genocide are dubious and tenuous, at best. And, while the people of Iraq suffered under the UN regime, it should be observed that Iraq, under the regime of Saddam Hussein, brought much greater misery to his own people. Accusations of genocide in Iraq, where they are made, should focus on Saddam's bloody regime, the *primum movens* (the initial stimulus) for the sanctions, rather than the sanctions themselves (Sassoon 2011).

THE COMPLEXITIES OF CLASSIFICATION

As can be seen, there are all manner of problems attached to defining genocide, and the term often is simply inappropriate when people seek to explain massive human evil resulting in the death of vast numbers of human beings. Clarifying what genocide is *not* is just as important as ensuring precision when confirming what it actually *is*, and it is vitally important that we get the terminology right. Quite clearly, we are dealing with a term carrying so much power that precision is needed when applying it. If anything can be incorporated or rejected as genocide according to individual preferences, then there is no certainty that we will ever be able to bring the intellectual rigour to the topic that serious academic scholarship demands.

As discussed in **Chapter 1**, the UN Convention on Genocide is highly flawed. It provides a definition that is in many ways unsatisfactory. The field can possibly be broadened, such as adding war-related deaths or gathering together all instances of massacre, area bombing, state-directed killing of large numbers of people, or mass destruction caused by other agencies or individuals.

Locating such actions within taxonomies of genocide can be useful, but only if an acceptable definition has also been agreed. And herein lies a problem: studying genocide with a view to eradicating it is a worthwhile task only if scholars can first agree on precisely what it is they are studying. And other than the inadequate definition in the UN Convention, there are no other universally accepted definitions of genocide. If the quest to understand genocide is to be more than just an abstract scholarly enterprise, it must be recalled that it is only through the United Nations that the countries of the world will ever apply themselves seriously to the question of confronting genocide. In the eyes of the international community, the UN definition is the only one from which prosecutions (and, therefore, responsibility) can be reached.

DISCUSSION QUESTIONS

- Why do you think the UN Convention on Genocide has embedded within it the idea of intent as a key factor?
- Why are some cases of massive human rights abuse not considered to be genocide?
- In view of the fact that people suffer and die at the hands of others, both in war and in peacetime, why do issues of definition regarding genocide matter so much?
- Looking over the examples given in this chapter, are there any that you would consider to be clear-cut cases of genocide? Why/why not?

9

THE DILEMMAS OF PREVENTION AND INTERVENTION

INHIBITIONS IN THE INTERNATIONAL SYSTEM

The wording in the formal title of the UN Convention on Genocide is clear: it requires both *prevention* and *punishment*. It places a clear premium on genocide prevention before punishment, in the expectation that by preventing genocide there will be no need to punish it.

There are, however, significant inhibitions built into the international system that militate against successful prevention initiatives. The twin tasks of preventing genocide before it occurs, and stopping it while it is underway, have (as the examples in this short volume have shown) not proven to be achievable. In a world of nation states, the prospect of effective interventionist action is slight, despite the experiences of the past century and the constantly expressed promise of "never again." Worthwhile change would not appear to be within easy reach unless the essential foundations of the international system undergo fundamental change, something that does not seem likely to happen in the foreseeable future.

STATE SOVEREIGNTY

The past century has witnessed massive human rights catastrophes that, all too frequently, have resulted in genocide. In nearly all these cases, there was next to nothing in the way of large-scale or effective intervention to stop the killing. The principle of state sovereignty, sacrosanct in international affairs ever since the 1648 Treaty of Westphalia, sees a global system in which nation states govern their own affairs free of interference from others (Jackson 2007). Accordingly, one state may not involve itself in the internal affairs of another, regardless of what happens there – whether that should be an unfavourable change of government, bloody mayhem, civil war, revolution, or genocide (Kegley and Raymond 2001).

Recent decades, given the post-Cold War humanitarian catastrophes since the 1990s, have seen challenges to the primacy of sovereignty. With increasing urgency, questions have been asked as to why genocide, ethnic cleansing, and large-scale crimes should go uncontested. As we have seen, in one case – that of Kosovo in 1999 – wholesale ethnic cleansing was avoided through unsanctioned unilateral military action. In another, in East Timor the same year, a further massive human rights disaster was averted through UN-approved multilateral action. Prevailing international norms have moved on to a new plane, rejecting the "anything goes" approach, suggesting that perhaps the cases of Kosovo and East Timor might have been early harbingers of things to come rather than an indication that full-scale change had actually arrived.

The key rests with the United Nations. Comprising sovereign states – indeed, established on the very principle of the maintenance of state sovereignty within a peaceful world – even UN membership is determined by the recognition of sovereignty. Today, there are no sovereign states in the world that are not UN members. The United Nations as an organisation, moreover, was set up in 1945 for the purpose of ensuring peace *between* states, not *within* them. This is important when considering United Nations intervention in international humanitarian crises, as it must be recognised that the reason for the existence of the UN is international peace, not stopping internal human rights violations. Further, statecraft demands that states must always look to their own interests before they contemplate what might be happening elsewhere, unless that poses a threat or a challenge. This interest-driven priority – looking at the world as it really is, rather than as it should be – is the fundamental difference between what we call realism and what might be termed "idealism." Nation states are dominated by the former; they can rarely afford the luxury of the latter (Bartrop 2013: 119–135).

We are thus forced to ask very weighty questions when it comes to genocide prevention: in a world dominated by sovereignty and *realpolitik* (that is, political realism), is intervention to stop genocide ever a serious option? Are there forms of intervention other than that of a physical or military nature? And finally, is the dominance of sovereignty likely to give way to a new system in which intervention in the internal affairs of other states is not only successful in stopping massive human rights abuses and genocide, but is also permissible and welcomed as the best way to proceed?

The German term *realpolitik* is employed by political scientists for the purpose of identifying the reasons behind certain state behaviours relative to other states. It effectively refers to an attitude whereby states do not have friends, but interests; accordingly, states work to secure those interests in a manner they find the least threatening, and from which they can derive the greatest possible advantage. Thus, *realpolitik* sees states assessing every situation in accordance with that situation's ultimate implications for state security, rather than with idealistic concerns that might place the state at risk.

Put slightly differently, the system sees states as neither moral nor immoral; rather, they are amoral, with all means – good and bad, ethical and unethical – viewed as legitimate in the pursuit of state security. Humanitarian initiatives, of "doing the right thing" in the face of evil, have until very recently not been a satisfactory reason for states breaking away from a *realpolitik* approach to international relations, particularly if as a result they might find themselves involved in physical confrontation with other states. Every state that wages war, no matter how powerful, must reckon on the possibility of defeat, a situation which in no way serves state interests.

The principle of state sovereignty is therefore the key to understanding how *realpolitik* works. Sovereignty, put simply, is the governing authority within a polity that renders a state independent and free from any form of external control. Sovereign control means that a state has the ability *and the right* to construct itself as its rulers (or, hopefully, its citizens) deem appropriate, without outside interference.

This rests, furthermore, on three unchallengeable principles: first, that the rights of all sovereign states are equal; second, that intervention by states within the domestic jurisdiction of others is impermissible; and third, that sovereign immunity – the protection a state is given from being sued in the courts of other states – is guaranteed. The implication is clear. Within its borders, a state rules supreme, and whatever it does within those borders constitutes its own internal business that should not be violated by another state (Jackson 2007).

EARLY INITIATIVES

Contesting this has never been easy, though efforts were made from the beginning of the twentieth century. An early start was found in the Hague Conventions of 1899 and 1907. These arose out of two international conferences called to discuss issues relating to the conduct of states at war. It was recognised that alternatives should be sought prior to conflict taking place, and that these could include such devices as disarmament and international arbitration. At its base was an attempt to try to diminish the evils of war by revising, wherever possible, the general laws and customs that had until then regulated the nature of conflict. The Conventions were signed by 26 states, who agreed to restrain their behaviour by delineating a set of actions that would, from now on, be classed as war crimes (Solis 2010: 51–57). While this was to be welcomed, the Conventions refrained from embracing the idea of any sort of international court, preferring to retreat behind well-established principles relating to state sovereignty. Moreover, nothing was developed in the way of an enforcement mechanism for states contravening the laws proscribed by the treaties.

In August 1914, the outbreak of the most extensive and destructive global conflict the world had seen to that time stymied earlier hopes. Shunning idealism, the Great Powers went to war as though the Hague Conventions had never been written. Interests of state dictated the pace of escalation, and throughout the conflict thoughts rarely turned to questions of human rights, the position of non-combatants, or war crimes, other than in the accusations levelled by one side against the other. Nonetheless, the principles embodied in the Conventions (and their forerunner, the Geneva Conventions) were invoked from time to time during the war.

As the war was drawing to an end, and as idealism came to the fore in such declarations as US President Woodrow Wilson's

(1856–1924) Fourteen Points (which included such principles as the evacuation and restoration of territories occupied by foreign powers, and the establishment of new states along the lines of "national self-determination"), the ideals upon which a more caring global community might be crafted were deliberated upon (Knock 1992). The creation in 1919 of the League of Nations, it was hoped by many, would see the realisation of such a community – the phoenix, perhaps, that would rise from the ashes of war.

The League was a radical experiment. In its attempts at creating a new global order based on open diplomacy, fairness, and the rule of law, it sought to reduce the risk of conflict through dialogue and negotiation, rather than through multilateral intervention (Henig 2010). But the League found itself a prisoner of the very features it was attempting to supersede. These included such factors as *realpolitik*, the states system, secret diplomacy, and the impunity of states acting in accordance with their own interests. Its major problem was that none of its members were ever prepared to surrender any portion of their sovereignty in favour of untried ideals. Thus, no new proposals involving peacemaking, peace enforcement, or peacekeeping were realistically suggested or tried. It took the failure of the League, followed by another World War between 1939 and 1945, and the subsequent creation of a new international organisation – the United Nations – to realise the necessity of cutting through the structures that had so impeded the League's earlier ability to act.

After the Second World War, new standards were developed that, rather than permitting international intervention to stop such phenomena as genocide and massive human rights violations, took responsibility for these acts away from states and placed them squarely at the feet of individuals. An example of this is to be found in the so-called Nuremberg Principles, a set of precepts adopted by the United Nations International Law Commission in 1950 (Totten and Bartrop 2008: 312–313). Their essential implication was that every person is responsible for their own actions and that, as a result, no one stands above international law, meaning that the defence of "following superior orders" would henceforth not be recognised unless an accused was acting under duress and there was no moral choice available. The Nuremberg Principles have since been incorporated into a number of multilateral treaties, most notably the Rome Statute of July 17, 1998 that would later, in 2002, establish the International Criminal Court.

The year 1948 saw the adoption of two vitally important initiatives pointing the way towards a new direction for humanitarian action: the UN Convention on Genocide (December 9, 1948), and the Universal Declaration of Human Rights (December 10, 1948). Coming just one day apart, their appearance signalled the determination of the member states to see to it that in the aftermath of the Holocaust the promise of "never again" would become a reality. Article 4 of the Convention on Genocide referred to the establishment of "such international penal tribunal as may have jurisdiction" for the purpose of trying cases of genocide, and, although it took half a century of constant effort, the signing of the Rome Statute in 1998 saw the notion of an international court become enshrined as international law. The treaty agreed that the key crimes to be addressed by the court, once established, would be genocide, crimes against humanity, and war crimes. It was agreed that the International Criminal Court would become operational after 60 of the signatory states had ratified their accession within their home legislatures (Schabas 2011; Bosco 2014).

The United Nations, of course, is indispensable in any discussion of human rights development and international legislation that is designed to make the world a safer place, and the Convention on Genocide is its most important contribution. On December 2, 1998, on the Convention's 50th anniversary, the General Assembly reaffirmed its significance through the adoption of a new resolution. Member states were invited to continue to review and assess the progress made in the Convention's implementation, and to identify obstacles and the way they could be overcome (http://www.un.org/News/Press/docs/1998/19981202.ga9523.html).

The most important of these, and arguably that which has the best potential to be realised in the future, resulted from an initiative taken in September 2000 by the government of Canada. In establishing the International Commission on Intervention and State Sovereignty, the Canadians started a process that led, in December 2001, to the appearance of a report entitled *The Responsibility to Protect*. It argued that the international community has a responsibility not only to prevent mass atrocities, but also to react to crisis situations through a variety of actions ranging from diplomacy, through coercion, to military intervention (ICISS 2001). Its principles were picked up, and at the UN World Summit held on September 14–16, 2005 representatives of member states agreed to adopt the Responsibility to Protect (R2P) initiative. This will be discussed in greater depth later in this chapter.

THE POWER OF *REALPOLITIK*

A fundamental truth in international affairs is that states will almost always assess how far they will involve themselves in the affairs of others according to the principles of *realpolitik*. Sometimes the rationales offered for particular actions do not make for pleasant reading, forming, as they do, the clearest expression of practical politics. Examples abound, from Britain's attitude towards Biafra in the late 1960s (Stremlau 1997), to that of the United States towards Cambodia throughout the 1970s (Shawcross 1979), Australia's position on East Timor between 1975 and 1999 (Fernandes 2005), and that of France towards Rwanda in the early 1990s (Wallis 2007; Kroslak 2007). Sometimes, policy positions are simply dictated through a callous disregard on the part of some policy makers for those in need, which is not necessarily the same as *realpolitik* but is all too often masked by it.

If *realpolitik* considerations usually determine the extent to which states will or will not intervene in genocide, it must be borne in mind that a number of possibilities do exist for successful intervention, though these do not necessarily involve military action. They might be softer options, but they can nonetheless be effective in at least showing other states that *realpolitik* can be transcended, that the sovereignty principle can be breached, and that intervention can take place without the risk of war or physical confrontation.

One possibility is to be found in the fostering of democracy as an effective stimulus for deterring the emergence of genocide. In what many political scientists describe as "soft power" (Nye 2004) – the ability to obtain one's policy objectives through persuading others to voluntarily follow one's own goals – there are ways in which an anti-genocide culture can be fostered by states in their relationships with others, without necessarily breaching sovereignty or putting themselves at risk due to *realpolitik* concerns (Weart 2000).

The idea of the "democratic peace" is one such notion. Put succinctly, the idea is that the more democratic the world is, the less likely it is that war and genocide will occur. The fostering of democracy, peacefully and gradually, is thereby advanced as a serious alternative to military intervention (Rummel 2002).

Attractive as this theory is, nonetheless it has its detractors. Critics of the democratic peace notion counter that many First World democracies are founded on a genocidal dispossession of indigenous populations, and that they have often elsewhere engaged in genocidal practices against other, less developed nations (Docker 2008). Intervention, though for many people an attractive notion, thus presents difficulties – particularly when some nations, with all the good will in the world, attempt to export democracy to undemocratic countries before they are prepared to receive it. Again, we are confronted by issues relating to *realpolitik*, as the export of democracy, though appealing, is an activity with which states must proceed very carefully lest war ensue despite (or because of) their best efforts. The recent wars in Iraq and Afghanistan, led by the United States, provide ideal examples of how imposing democracy onto societies not prepared to accept it can lead to unforeseen and destructive outcomes.

Notwithstanding the fact that the international community and individual states have engaged in interventionist activities to stop massive human rights violations, *realpolitik* concerns always play a key role with regard to who, when, where, and why intervention will take place, and what form it will take. India, for example, only intervened to stop the killing in Bangladesh in 1971 when the tide of refugees assumed critical levels, not especially out of a desire to stop the killing for its own sake (Bass 2013). Similarly, Vietnam invaded Pol Pot's Democratic Kampuchea in January 1979 because the Khmer Rouge was running amok and Pol Pot's paranoia had led him to authorise extensive cross-border incursions (Kiernan 2008). Vietnam did not invade in order to drive out a genocidal regime, but in order to neutralise a threat to its security – a classic *realpolitik* scenario. Tanzanian President Julius Nyerere (1922–99) operated in exactly the same way after Uganda's genocidal dictator, Idi Amin (c. 1925–2003), invaded Tanzania in 1978 (Acheson-Brown 2001).

Such actions have little to do with humanitarianism other than as a by-product. Furthermore, with the onset of the crisis situations of the 1990s in Bosnia and Rwanda, multilateral interventions authorised by the United Nations often took on the character of ignominious debacles rather than successful campaigns. Too often, UN peacekeeping missions were unable to obtain satisfactory logistical or manpower support, were the subject of countless debates that did not produce action, or found their mandates weakened progressively (or started out weak to begin with). And all these stemmed, in one way or another, from issues stemming from *realpolitik* and concerns about state sovereignty.

There are no easy answers to the question of how intervention to stop genocide should take place. Physical intervention in the form of military action can be effective, but states that engage in such action not only must look to their own interests before acting; they are also inevitably required by the international community to enforce their will in accordance with approval from the United Nations, lest they be held up as aggressors acting unilaterally and illegally. Furthermore, states engaging in military intervention must be fully prepared for all contingencies, good and bad, and possess a necessary commitment to see their assignment fulfilled – something that is often difficult when casualties occur and democratic governments have to explain them to a sceptical voting public.

If considered from a wide-angle perspective, absolute sovereignty has become weaker since the end of the Cold War, particularly as it applies to state perpetration of crimes against humanity and genocide. The human rights movement has provided a firm foundation for responsive actions in the aftermath of genocide. However, when it comes to resolutions to stop genocide in the UN General Assembly or Security Council, states for the most part still consider their vital national interests ahead of humanitarian intervention, afraid of showing the necessary commitment that could bring about real, effective, and lasting impacts.

THE RESPONSIBILITY TO PROTECT

The hope implanted within the Responsibility to Protect (R2P) initiative suggests that the leaders of an increasing number of states do see a role for the state to play in the future. The wording of R2P's paragraphs 138 and 139 leaves little room for doubt on this

(http://www.un.org/en/preventgenocide/adviser/pdf/World%20Su
mmit%20Outcome%20Document.pdf#page=30):

> 138. Each individual State has the responsibility to protect its populations
> from genocide, war crimes, ethnic cleansing and crimes against
> humanity. This responsibility entails the prevention of such crimes,
> including their incitement, through appropriate and necessary means.
> We accept that responsibility and will act in accordance with it. The
> international community should, as appropriate, encourage and help
> States to exercise this responsibility and support the United Nations in
> establishing an early warning capability.
>
> 139. The international community, through the United Nations, also
> has the responsibility to use appropriate diplomatic, humanitarian and
> other peaceful means, in accordance with Chapters VI and VIII of the
> Charter, to help protect populations from genocide, war crimes, ethnic
> cleansing and crimes against humanity. In this context, we are prepared
> to take collective action, in a timely and decisive manner, through the
> Security Council, in accordance with the Charter, including Chapter VII,
> on a case-by-case basis and in cooperation with relevant regional
> organizations as appropriate, should peaceful means be inadequate and
> national authorities manifestly fail to protect their populations from
> genocide, war crimes, ethnic cleansing and crimes against humanity. We
> stress the need for the General Assembly to continue consideration of
> the responsibility to protect populations from genocide, war crimes,
> ethnic cleansing and crimes against humanity and its implications,
> bearing in mind the principles of the Charter and international law. We
> also intend to commit ourselves, as necessary and appropriate, to
> helping States build capacity to protect their populations from genocide,
> war crimes, ethnic cleansing and crimes against humanity and to assisting
> those which are under stress before crises and conflicts break out.

By January 2009, the R2P idea had developed to the point where
UN Secretary-General Ban Ki-moon (b. 1944) released a new
report entitled *Implementing the Responsibility to Protect*. This, in turn,
led to a debate in the General Assembly in July 2009 that discussed
the whole concept. While most of the 94 representatives who
spoke on behalf of their states expressed support for R2P, a great
many were conscious of the problems it raised regarding sovereignty and fulfilling its ideals in the reality of crisis situations. The

recommendations made had already addressed the sovereignty idea, however, noting that in the first instance each individual state has the responsibility to protect its *own* population from genocide, war crimes, ethnic cleansing, and crimes against humanity. Only when this was not happening, and after the international community (through the United Nations) had tried to protect populations at risk using appropriate diplomatic, humanitarian, and other peaceful means, would the signatories to R2P be authorised to take collective action, in a timely and decisive manner, through the Security Council. Should a state either allow massive human rights violations to occur, or be committing them itself, a case could then be put that the state was not acting in a manner appropriate to sovereignty, and that it deserved to have action taken against it (Evans 2008).

Despite these arguments, a critic of R2P could still argue that the initiative infringes the sovereignty principle. By reference to the United Nations Security Council, any action invoking R2P would need *de facto* support from the Council's Permanent Members, who might or might not agree based on a reading of what their own interests are in the situation. The real test of this new-found commitment will come when the states that have agreed to take on the obligations enshrined in R2P are actually required to engage in actions to stop genocide. Until then, in light of the record of the past century, these principles must remain a theoretical – though thoroughly laudable – pipe-dream.

If multilateral action in a world of nation states does not always translate into the saving of lives when the realities of statecraft are invoked, are cases of unilateral action any better? The NATO intervention in Kosovo in 1999 was successful in its avowed aim of stemming the likelihood of genocide and permanent ethnic cleansing. Even though the intervention was an action illegal in international law, and it cost innocent civilian lives to bring it about, it nonetheless did bring violent Serbian actions against the Kosovar Albanians to an end (Weymouth and Henig 2001).

The overall question is not an easy one to answer: should the primacy of international law remain and due process be adhered to while people are dying; or should big states go after small villains and thereby save lives, regardless of whether or not there is international approval to do so? As the twenty-first century is unfolding, the answers are far from clear.

For the most part, when discussions have taken place either as to why members of the international community have not attempted to prevent genocide or why interventions have been so ineffective, explanations have centred either on the lack of "political will" or concerns related to *realpolitik* – both of which are, of course, intimately related in any case. There is, however, another reason, and that is the simple but profound fact that many state and inter-governmental politicians and bureaucrats have often simply not cared enough about certain crisis situations to take firm action. This, while not dealing with international behaviour directly, introduces a vital human dimension to our considerations, and is a factor which must never be overlooked.

While states are not people – and thus do not "think" or "feel" or "believe" as people do – their behaviour is nonetheless *managed* by people who can, and frequently do, bring their thoughts, feelings, and beliefs to the table when policy options are being formulated. Too often this has translated into insensitivity, indifference, and sometimes even antipathy towards the formation of state policies based on the principle of "doing the right thing." Frequently, as well, sovereignty has trumped the moral considerations of those seeking imaginative policy directions founded on principles of ethical goodness in the face of obvious expressions of state-driven malevolence. Clearly, there is still a great deal of work to be done concerning human morality before the safety of the world's citizens can be guaranteed.

It is not certain that a way can soon be found to resolve the dilemma between state sovereignty and *realpolitik* on the one hand, and intervention to stop genocide on the other, unless there is a significant measure of rethinking the issue at the UN and an accompanying set of reforms that will cut through the centuries-old principles that regard the primacy of the state as sacrosanct. The advent of R2P has made an impressive start into this new way of looking at things, but there is still a long way to go. States remain fearful of abandoning *realpolitik*, a principle that has dominated state actions since the seventeenth century. Major transformations must take place in the manner in which states interact with each other if they are committed to the creation of a genocide-free world. Leaders need to reconsider how they can act for humanitarian purposes without risking their countries' security. Anything short of this will be inadequate.

While it is true that the genocidal events of the twentieth century saw a slow wearing down of the sanctity of state sovereignty, the pace of that process was not rapid enough to save millions of lives. Looked at from a purely pragmatic perspective, perhaps there was no reason to expect anything else. The first decade of the twenty-first century saw the onset of unprecedented global terror in the aftermath of the 9/11 attacks on the United States; increasing fears relating to global warming and sustainable development; ongoing energy crises in various parts of the world; and the global financial crisis that hit world markets after September 2008, disrupting credit, banking, currency, and trade throughout the globe. It could be said that any one of these was just as important for the future as the spectre of genocide, and they were, for many people in the First World, more immediate and had a deeper impact. Put simply, genocide has to compete for attention in the corridors of power, and, owing to its moral/humanitarian nature, there is always a likelihood that state interests will place a lower value on the saving of human lives in places far away, than with addressing pressing issues closer to home.

When decisions concerning the handling of genocide situations *are* made in the future, they will have to be made with firmness, a willingness to see the objectives through no matter what gets in the way (and this includes the resolution to absorb casualties), and the cooperation of *all* international actors.

It would be easy to remain pessimistic in all of this. History has given little reason to presume that the sovereignty principle will be completely overthrown soon, or that the world's states will come together in a spirit of harmony for the good of all humanity. Until now, the global system has simply not worked that way, nor was it constructed such that it could go easily down that path. When states finally recognise that their vital national interests are in fact served by working together to stop the curse of genocide, perhaps real, effective, and lasting change for the better can take place. And that, truly, would herald the start of a brave new world.

DISCUSSION QUESTIONS

- Should the sovereign immunity of states be respected at all times, regardless of the actions they take with respect to their own citizens?

- Do you think that initiatives such as Responsibility to Protect are likely to succeed in the long term?
- In your view, should states act without United Nations approval in order to stop genocide, if such approval is slow in coming or not sanctioned?
- What should happen when a state rejects the moral standards of modern society and starts to engage in genocide against its own people?

10

INTERNATIONAL JUSTICE

JUSTICE AND GENOCIDE

When do genocides end? As with so many areas in the study of genocide, there is no clear-cut answer to this question. For some, the response is simple: genocide ends when the killing stops. For others, the phenomenon that is genocide embraces a wide range of what might be termed "closure issues." Stopping the killing and finding a way to ensure it does not recommence is obviously important, as is keeping the peace; but bringing the perpetrators to justice is one of the keys to ensuring both closure and, from the depths of despair, a means to ensure some sort of graduated return to a form of familiar life.

Can justice be met? In the aftermath of genocide, injured societies undergo a range of experiences as they seek to regain some measure of normalcy. These can include a quest for justice; reintegration into the international community; a degree of comity with the victim society's neighbours; nation building, or, in a majority of cases, nation *re*building; psychological counselling on a massive scale; and physical reconstruction of the social and economic infrastructure in light of what is invariably enormous material destruction. But bringing the perpetrators to justice can make all the difference between a satisfactory confrontation with the recent past, or a longer, more painful and traumatic crisis that can keep the country in ruins and destabilise the region in which it is located (Smith 2009; Clark and Kaufman 2009).

This, of course, is a highly generalised picture, subject to variations across continents, states, and regions. What is common to one situation does not necessarily apply to another, yet a single point of commonality does touch all cases: a desire on the part of the victimised peoples to try to return to as "normal" a life as possible, to the degree that this can be achieved.

Those who have lost everything need to know that those responsible for the massive upheaval through which they have suffered and survived will be brought to book for what they have done. Indeed, they have a right to demand it if they are to move ahead. But the question must always be asked: how is justice to be achieved? For many years it seemed as though this question would remain unanswered; even today the situation remains incomplete and unresolved.

Efforts have been made throughout the past century to find ways to create appropriate mechanisms that serve the needs of justice and safeguard the rights of the accused. The international community has sought to establish impartial tribunals that over-ride the temptation to establish kangaroo courts, but this has been a slow process that has, of necessity, meant that the law has had to evolve. Moreover, in the creation of such an environment, genocide did not even start out as the primary category of crime.

THE NUREMBERG TRIALS

On November 20, 1945 the trial of major Nazi war criminals at Nuremberg began, its fundamental intention being to punish those members of Germany's Nazi government and High Command for having led the world into war and perpetrating innumerable horrors against those caught in the Nazi net. A secondary ambition was to set in place a legal precedent for dealing with any future violations of the world's peace, a peace the new United Nations organisation was committed to upholding. The trial was to be the first in history held for crimes committed against the peace of the world (Taylor 1992; Conot 1993).

The basis of the trials was laid out on August 8, 1945 when the four powers of France, Britain, the Soviet Union, and the United

States signed the London Charter after a conference determined the charges that would be brought against the captured Nazi leaders now that the war had ended. These included crimes against peace, war crimes, and crimes against humanity.

When the International Military Tribunal (IMT), based in the German city of Nuremberg, sat for the purpose of trying 22 major Nazis in November 1945, the accused were charged under any of four counts:

1 the "Common Plan" – that is, taking part in conspiracy to commit crimes against the peace, war crimes, and crimes against humanity;
2 crimes against peace – that is, participating in the planning and waging of wars of aggression in violation of international treaties and agreements;
3 war crimes – that is, murder and ill-treatment of civilians in occupied territory or on the high seas, deportations for slave labour, murder or ill-treatment of war prisoners, killing of hostages, plunder, exacting collective penalties, wanton destruction and devastation, conscription of civilian labour, forcing civilians to swear allegiance to a hostile power, and "Germanisation" of occupied territories; and
4 crimes against humanity – that is, murder, extermination, enslavement, deportation, other inhumane acts committed against civilian populations before the war and during the war, and persecution on political, religious, and racial grounds in the common plan mentioned in count 1. (Smith 1981)

These trials were to set the tone for all subsequent war crimes trials down to the present day (Ehrenfreund 2007; Ball 1999).

The major emphasis of the IMT lay in a concern to bring to justice those who had upset the international order by waging aggressive war, not those who had exclusively committed egregious acts of barbarity. Ever since Nuremberg, however – and with an increasing tempo – an impression has developed that the trials had, as their major focus, something to do with the Holocaust and the other atrocities committed by the Nazis. Indeed, while these events did in fact form a major part of the indictments, and were specifically covered in count 4 (crimes against humanity), it is important to record that the IMT was not established in order to punish the leaders of the Third Reich for the Holocaust. On the contrary, the main intention of Nuremberg was to try those who were held to have been responsible for bringing about the Second World War, and to hold them accountable for the damage and loss of life that had been caused as a result of it.

Because of the shocking nature of the revelations made about atrocities committed against Jews, however, from an early date Nuremberg came to be seen first and foremost as a tribunal judging the anti-human evils perpetrated by the Third Reich. The indictment relating to crimes against humanity rapidly became the count that most clearly represented the abhorrence held by people around the world at what they understood Nazism to mean.

It is worthwhile considering, for a moment, the four indictments. The first – the "Common Plan" – was in reality a general indictment summarising the other three, and charged the accused with engaging in a conspiracy to commit them. The second – crimes against peace – charged the accused with causing the war that had just been fought. Only in counts 3 and 4 – war crimes and crimes against humanity, respectively – was the human dimension to the Nazis' wrongdoing introduced. Graphic though they are, the issues specified in counts 3 and 4 were secondary to the Tribunal's primary aim, namely the punishment of those found guilty for the planning and waging of aggressive war as stipulated in count 2.

Nuremberg should thus be seen as more than a trial sitting in judgment on the Holocaust. Nothing was seen in the first instance as being more criminal than the foisting of aggressive war upon a world that had previously been clearly committed to avoiding it. Yet the alignment of Jewish horrors with the IMT was more and more apparent as each new day dawned. News of Nazi atrocities was broadcast all over the world, and rapidly became the central motif justifying Nuremberg. Its main effect would be to see the Tribunal perceived as a trial for the Holocaust, with the main reason – the planning and waging of aggressive war – falling by the wayside.

When the IMT (comprised of two judges each from Britain, France, the United States, and the Soviet Union) handed down its decisions, six of the accused were found guilty on all four counts, and sentenced to hang; another six were similarly sentenced after having been found guilty of some of the counts. Others received long prison sentences ranging from ten years to life, while three were acquitted and (after some delay) released.

There was no doubt that Nuremberg resulted in landmark judgments. Never before had such an international tribunal of victor nations sat to deliver verdicts over a vanquished foe, and never before had there been such a vast set of compromises made across often competing legal systems in order to reach a convergence of opinion. In the aftermath of the IMT, another 12 separate trials took place, also at Nuremberg, between 1946 and 1949. These considered the fates of the SS as a criminal organisation, Nazi physicians who had conducted medical experiments against prisoners, *Kommandants* of Nazi concentration camps, leaders of major business enterprises, and the like (Priemel and Stiller 2012). In total, 177 persons were convicted and sentenced either to death or terms of imprisonment.

While the Holocaust itself was not on trial, nonetheless the revelations that came as a result served to confirm for people living in the Allied countries why the struggle against the Nazis had been too important to lose. The Charter of the IMT was unprecedented in international law, and a vital step on the road to a universal antigenocide, anti-crimes against humanity, and anti-war crimes regime that would be binding upon all. This would see its crowning moment (to date) in 2002, with the establishment of the International Criminal Court in The Hague.

INTERNATIONAL MILITARY TRIBUNAL FOR THE FAR EAST

The International Military Tribunal for the Far East (IMTFE), also known as the Tokyo War Crimes Tribunal, was convened on April 29, 1946, and adjourned on November 12, 1948. Its task was to try the leaders of Japan for three types of war crimes: Class A crimes related to those who participated in a joint conspiracy to start and wage war; Class B crimes related to those who committed crimes against humanity; and Class C crimes related to those in command positions who planned and ordered (or failed to prevent) war crimes and crimes against humanity (Totani 2008).

The indictments charged the defendants with conquering territories in such a manner that murder, maiming, and ill-treatment of prisoners of war and civilian internees was the norm, where they would be forced to work under inhumane conditions. They were also accused of plunder, of wantonly destroying cities, towns and villages, and of committing mass murder, rape, torture, and other barbaric acts against the populations over which they had control.

The trials were held in the War Ministry office in Tokyo, and extended over a period of two and a half years. Of the 80 Class A suspects, 28 were actually brought to trial. Two of the 28 defendants died of natural causes during the trial. One had a mental breakdown on the first day of trial, was sent to a psychiatric ward, and was released in 1948. The remaining 25 were all found guilty, many on multiple counts. Seven were sentenced to death by hanging, 16 to life imprisonment, and two to lesser terms. All seven sentenced to death were found to be guilty of inciting, or otherwise implicated in, mass atrocities. Of those indicted for Class B and Class C war crimes, some 5,700 were tried, with nearly 1,000 condemned to death for crimes committed against nationals of several of the Allied countries (Cryer and Boister 2008; Brackman 1987).

While the IMT at Nuremberg was viewed by most in Europe as being a legitimate expression of the Allies' determination to serve justice, the IMTFE bore accusations of dubious legitimacy from the start, with many claims being made of "victor's justice" and a racially based revenge motive (Minear 1971). Like Nuremberg, however, the trials did have a concern with crimes against humanity and war crimes, and the deliberations at Tokyo added to the case law that could be called upon in later years when allegations of genocide in other parts of the world were introduced (Maga 2001).

POST-WAR DEVELOPMENTS

The Latin concept of *Jus in Bello*, or "laws during the waging of war," is the humanitarian law dealing with the conduct of war (Byers 2005). It demands that states at war must make a clear distinction between non-combatants and combatants. Several of the international legal instruments that had been in the process of development since the Geneva and Hague Conventions had taken account of this notion, but it was only as a result of the horrors of the Second World War that any serious attention was given to the status and protection of civilians in wartime.

On December 9, 1948, of course, the UN General Assembly resolved that genocide is a crime under international law, and called on member states to undertake an international effort for its prevention and punishment. What is often overlooked is that, the day after the Convention on Genocide was passed, the UN made another landmark declaration: the UN Universal Declaration of Human Rights. This historic document consists of a Preamble and 30 Articles. Among the topics addressed are slavery, torture, access to the legal systems of one's own country, privacy, residency and movement, the right to marry, the right to own property, freedom of thought and opinion, participation in the governmental process, the right to work, access to education, and the right to share in one's own culture (Morsink 2000). The Universal Declaration of Human Rights constitutes an essential foundation for international human rights legislation, though it must be remembered that it is a declaration rather than (as with the Convention on Genocide) a binding piece of international legislation. States that sign on to it are not bound to act on its provisions (though their accession usually looks good for reasons of domestic consumption).

What *is* binding, however, is accession to the International Court of Justice (ICJ), the principal judicial organ of the United Nations, established in 1945. Its express purpose is to settle legal disputes between states and provide advice to the United Nations on international legal questions (Kolb 2013). As such, the ICJ does not hear cases involving private individuals or international non-governmental organisations. With this in mind, the ICJ is not a tribunal established to prosecute individuals for genocide, crimes against humanity, or war crimes. Only a state can bring an action, and this can only be against another state. Where genocide is concerned, this has happened on two occasions: Bosnia and Herzegovina vs. Serbia and Montenegro (case 91, judgment returned on February 26, 2007), and Croatia vs. Serbia. For the most part, humanitarian issues are not within the court's purview (Tams and Sloan 2013).

YUGOSLAVIA AND RWANDA

In 1993 and late 1994 respectively, the UN Security Council set up international courts to try the perpetrators of heinous crimes in the former Yugoslavia and Rwanda. While not entirely unprecedented, the new tribunals forced the first prosecutor, the South A.. Richard Goldstone (b. 1938), to instigate a range of strategies for the prosecution of those alleged to have committed genocide, crimes against humanity, and war crimes. To do so, he proceeded from the precedents set at the Nuremberg Trials, but also added new techniques appropriate to the late twentieth century such as the use of modern technology, provision for the calling of so-called "secret" witnesses, and the extension of the parameters of the crimes in question, such as securing the recognition of rape as a war crime under the Geneva Conventions.

The first of these new courts was the International Criminal Tribunal for the former Yugoslavia, or ICTY, established by the UN Security Council on May 25, 1993. Its broad scope covers the conflicts accompanying the dissolution of the Federal Republic of Yugoslavia between 1991 and 1999, and has jurisdiction over four clusters of crimes: grave breaches of the Geneva Conventions; violations of the laws and customs of war; genocide; and crimes against humanity. In view of the fact that the UN opposes the death penalty, the maximum sentence it can impose is life imprisonment.

The origin of the ICTY lay in an initial proposal from German Foreign Minister Klaus Kinkel (b. 1936), who was committed to finding a way to end the atrocities committed during the Yugoslav wars. UN Security Council Resolution 808 (February 22, 1993) then began to work on the creation of such a tribunal, with the intention of placing pressure on the leaders of the warring parties to cease their belligerent activities. Resolution 827, formally creating the ICTY, was the result (Hazan 2004).

The ICTY sits in The Hague. It was never intended that it would become a permanent tribunal, and will be wound up when it is considered by the UN that its work is complete. (As of this writing, it is anticipated that this should be some time in 2016.) The ICTY was the first war crimes court created by the UN and the first international war crimes tribunal since the Nuremberg and Tokyo tribunals. Its primary objective, through bringing perpetrators to trial, is to deter future crimes and to render justice to thousands of victims and their families. In this way, it not only contributes to a lasting peace in the former Yugoslavia, but also provides a climate in which the notion of international humanitarian justice becomes entrenched globally.

As if to underscore the idea that impunity will no longer be possible, the ICTY has indicted heads of state, prime ministers, army chiefs-of-staff, cabinet ministers, and many other high- and mid-level political, military, and police leaders from various parties to the Yugoslav conflicts (Kerr 2004). Most cases have dealt with alleged crimes committed by Serbs and Bosnian Serbs, but the Tribunal has investigated and brought charges against persons from every background involved in the conflicts of the former Yugoslavia.

A hallmark of the ICTY's operations has been its commitment to judicial impartiality, seeking at all times to exercise efficient and transparent international justice. Judges and officials are drawn from a pool of prominent international jurists, none of whom have been a party to any of the conflicts or groups from which the accused or accusers originate.

For all that, the ICTY began operations with serious budgetary and administrative setbacks. Costs outpaced the income of the court; reviewing evidence in preparation for each trial proved time consuming; and each trial got stalled through repeated postponements or recesses. Most troublesome was the process of locating and detaining those indicted; their arrest frequently depended on the cooperation of the governments of Bosnia-Herzegovina, Croatia, and, particularly, Serbia. The court has no extraterritorial jurisdiction with the power to send in officers to arrest accused people in countries that refuse to give them up, which has meant that many of those indicted have lived out their lives out of the Tribunal's reach (Schabas 2006).

Despite these obstacles, the court has managed to convict many indicted war criminals and bring others to trial, the most notable of which was the trial of the former president of Serbia, Slobodan Milošević (Armatta 2010). As the first head of state ever accused and tried for genocide, this was an unprecedented step in judicial history. In this sense, the Tribunal has irreversibly changed the landscape of international humanitarian law, but it has also extended case law by adding precedent-setting decisions on genocide, war crimes, and crimes against humanity. The Tribunal has established a new norm in conflict resolution, namely that leaders suspected of genocide and massive human rights violations will ultimately face justice if indicted and captured (Waters 2014).

While the Bosnian War was taking place, of course, the Rwandan Genocide broke out during the 100 days of madness between April and July, 1994. On November 9, 1994, UN Security Council Resolution 955 authorised the establishment of the International Criminal Tribunal for Rwanda (ICTR), a court similar in structure and purpose to the ICTY and following its lead in many areas. The two tribunals share a common judicial bench, though the ICTR sits in Arusha, Tanzania. Also like the ICTY, the ICTR is comprised of a tribunal of eminent judges from a wide range of countries, is truly international in scope, and is inspired by an open and transparent appeals procedure (Cruvellier 2010).

The ICTR, like its European counterpart, had major funding and infrastructural problems at the start, and was severely lacking in even the most fundamental requirements to investigate and bring prosecutions. Not only was a judicial infrastructure to be built from scratch, but supporters of the court also faced scepticism from member states of the UN, as well as outright opposition from members of the international legal community, many of whom questioned the legitimacy of such tribunals within international law.

Nonetheless, not only did the Tribunal commence and complete actions against alleged *génocidaires*, it also extended the case law of genocide. The trial of the former mayor of the commune of Taba, Jean-Paul Akayesu (b. 1953), was the first in history held specifically for the crime of genocide. On September 2, 1998, he was found guilty on nine of the 15 counts with which he was charged regarding genocide and crimes against humanity, making him the first person convicted of the crime of genocide in an internationally accredited courtroom – and thus the first occasion on which the UN Convention on Genocide was upheld as law (Akhavan 2013; Jones 2010). It was a landmark decision also in that it recognised the crime of rape as a form of genocide, and made the legal definition of rape more precise.

Other precedents established by the ICTR emerged in the trial of former Rwandan Prime Minister Jean Kambanda (b. 1955). Kambanda, who pleaded guilty to the crime of genocide (and was the first accused to do so in any international setting), was the first head of government to be convicted for this crime.

The maximum sentence that can be given through the ICTR is life imprisonment. Those convicted to terms of imprisonment are incarcerated in other African countries outside of Rwanda. The one exception has been the Belgian-born Georges Ruggiu (b. 1957), who worked for Hutu hate radio station RTLM. Found guilty in 2000 of incitement to commit genocide and crimes against humanity, he was sentenced to 12 years' imprisonment, to be served in Italy. He was granted an early release by Italian authorities, in controversial circumstances, in 2009 (Bartrop 2012: 280–281).

The ICTR is not the only means by which justice has been sought in Rwanda, though it is the only international court presiding over the events of 1994. Within Rwanda, pursuant to a new post-genocide law (Organic Law no. 08/96, dated August 30, 1996), special national trial chambers were set up specifically for the purpose of dealing with alleged *génocidaires*, as it was felt that courts existing prior to 1994 did not have the legal competence to try cases related to genocide and crimes against humanity. The death penalty was on the table, and applied in several cases. Rwanda finally abolished capital punishment in 2007.

A final form of post-genocide justice in Rwanda was *gacaca*, an indigenous form of local justice. The name is derived from the Kinyarwanda word *guacaca*, meaning grass; hence, *gacaca* is "justice on the grass." This is explained through the practice of the session taking place, during the pre-colonial period, out in the open.

The widespread use of *gacaca* courts in Rwanda was a direct response to the large number of prisoners – almost exclusively Hutu – who were taken into custody in the aftermath of the genocide. Owing to the massive devastation wrought on the legal and bureaucratic infrastructure of the country, the Western justice system previously introduced by Belgian colonial rule was completely destroyed. As scores of thousands of alleged *génocidaires* awaiting trial languished in hopelessly cramped conditions in Rwandan jails, a system of trial or release had to be found that would serve natural justice for both victims and accused. The introduction of *gacaca* in March 2001 was designed to deal with this problem (Clark 2011).

The system saw a judiciary comprised of leading members of a community known as "persons of integrity," regarded as *Inyangamugayo* or "uncorrupted." For the most part, they would be elected by their peers, and provided with the rudiments of state law through a number of government-run workshops. *Gacaca* law was not an adversarial system, whereby defendants and plaintiffs would have lawyers acting on their behalf. Rather, anyone present could speak in respect of an accused person, either for or against them; could interject to correct testimony or recollection; and could raise new issues pertaining to the accused. The major purpose of *gacaca*, other than for justice to be done (and to be seen to be done), was to work towards reconciliation and expedite judicial procedures against the accused. Where charges directly relating to the genocide were concerned, *gacaca* courts could impose custodial sentences, though not capital punishment.

THE INTERNATIONAL CRIMINAL COURT

The two International Criminal Tribunals – for Yugoslavia and Rwanda – were created as *ad hoc* courts not intended to be permanent. The idea of a more enduring tribunal, however, was something that had been long discussed. It had its origins in the nineteenth century, when a Swiss jurist, Gustave Moynier (1826–1910), suggested the need for such a tribunal to uphold the Geneva Convention of 1864. The concept was thereafter raised on a number of occasions, and found ultimate expression when the UN General Assembly adopted the Convention on Genocide. Article 4 of the Convention referred specifically to the establishment of "such international penal tribunal as may have jurisdiction" for the purpose of trying cases of genocide.

Various preparatory committees met throughout the 1990s to establish the form that such a court would take, and to draft the proposals on which the states attending its establishment would vote. At its 52nd session, the General Assembly decided that a "Diplomatic Conference of Plenipotentiaries on the Establishment of an International Criminal Court" would take place in Rome starting on June 15, 1998, and during the conference it was agreed that the key crimes the court would address would be genocide, crimes against humanity, and war crimes. No such universal tribunal existed until the resulting Rome Statute authorised the creation of one, and when it was adopted by 120 member states on July 17, 1998 it was, indeed, a historic day. It was agreed that the court would become operational after 60 of the signatories had ratified their accession within their home legislatures, and this was achieved in April, 2002 (Schabas 2011).

The ICC is located in The Hague, which has, over time, become the *de facto* centre of international human rights law and tribunals. It is intended to complement existing national judicial systems, and may only exercise its jurisdiction when national courts are unwilling or unable to investigate or prosecute such crimes. As such, it is the first permanent, treaty-based international court established to help end impunity for the perpetrators of massive human rights violations.

While the court is still young, it has already been very active. It has issued public indictments and arrest warrants (including the most high-profile, against Sudan's Omar Hassan Ahmad al-Bashir); several of those indicted have been detained, and are either awaiting trial or facing proceedings already.

OTHER TRIBUNALS

A number of other tribunals, established under international authority, have addressed the issue of genocide. Examples of these include the UN-supported Extraordinary Chambers in the Courts of Cambodia (ECCC), established in 1997 to try the leading members of the former Khmer Rouge regime in Cambodia for crimes against humanity, war crimes, and genocide; the Iraq Special Tribunal for Crimes against Humanity (IST), established by the Iraqi Governing Council (with Security Council oversight) in December 2003 for the purpose of bringing to justice Iraqis accused of war crimes, crimes against humanity, and genocide under the regime of Iraqi dictator Saddam Hussein; and the Special Court for Sierra Leone (SCSL), set up by the government of Sierra Leone and the United Nations for the purpose of prosecuting those bearing responsibility for serious violations of international humanitarian law committed in Sierra Leone after November 30, 1996.

Post-genocide justice mechanisms have often been unsuccessful, but where prosecutions have led to convictions the impact has been significant. The twin tasks of punishment and deterrence, always the most important indicators of justice being both done and seen to be done, have often served the purpose of genocide prevention. These mechanisms make genocide an activity that leaders of harsh regimes should avoid. In an ideal world, a person charged with the crime of genocide will, from that moment on, face many restrictions: if they are shielded by their home country, they can no longer move or travel overseas; they can no longer engage in the political process; they will, in all likelihood, lose their support base through negative publicity (nor will they have the ready access to the media that they once might have had); and, without recourse to all these things, their income stream might well plummet. In addition, there is also the stigma attached to having been indicted for the crime of genocide, resulting in a loss of face from which many careers could never hope to recover.

In short, while the problems attached to post-genocide justice are many and complex, there is enough to suggest that, if pursued resolutely by the international community in the years ahead, new forms of anti-genocide regulation might well serve the purpose of bringing home the message that genocide is a revolting practice that is ultimately self-defeating (Hirsch 2002).

DISCUSSION QUESTIONS

- Are efforts to create an anti-genocide legal regime likely to succeed?
- To what extent do you think that the IMT and the IMTFE were "victors' courts," that could not possibly hope to dispense impartial justice?
- Were the ICTY and ICTR simple face-saving exercises on the part of the Western countries in light of their failures to stop the genocides over which the courts were now presiding?
- Should the scope of the ICJ be expanded to include the actions of heads of state or leaders of governments?
- Do you think that accession to the ICC should be a condition of membership of the United Nations?

11

THE FUTURE

Will genocide feature as a critical factor in the world's future? Indeed, will the future be any different from the past? If evil people are more dedicated to the achievement of their evil ambitions than good people are to stopping them, what does that mean when it comes to saving lives and stopping the killing?

Genocide was the twentieth century's greatest ongoing human catastrophe, arguably a greater calamity than environmental degradation or nuclear proliferation. It is a worse disaster than war, with which it is often linked but from which it can be separated (Goldhagen 2009). Genocide addresses questions of how people perceive one another, and influences their behaviour when they interact. It conceives of humanity's future in light of how some people view themselves – superior, intelligent, vibrant, and perfectible – and to attain that future large numbers of so-called "surplus humans" have been slaughtered (Rubenstein 1983). Regimes around the world have tried to achieve their vision on tens of millions of corpses.

Genocide does not just emerge out of nowhere. In all cases there are always a number of preventable preliminary steps on the road to the ultimate "solution" of a regime's "problem." Such steps invariably involve processes of identification, alienation, isolation, and oppression, prior to the decisive stage of a target group's destruction. The twentieth century saw the continued refinement of such processes: introduced by the Ottoman Turks, refined by the Nazis, and developed across the rest of the century and into the new millennium.

All cases of genocide stem from a long-standing obsession on the part of the perpetrators with the physical, political, social, psychological, religious, or cultural differences of the victim group – differences perceived to be so great and irreconcilable that the perpetrators can see no other solution than an elimination of "the other" through total destruction. The objectives of those who shaped the post-1945 agenda increasingly became diluted as the twentieth century wore on, until the promise of "never again" rang hollow.

In light of this – and the realities of history – we are faced with the question of how all this is to be interpreted. If the trend over the course of the past century has been towards a greater likelihood than ever before that groups will be singled out for destruction, what hope does this offer those with a commitment to peace and the sanctity of life?

There is, unfortunately, no ready-made answer. Genocide still exists, despite the legal processes that have been instituted against it. The twentieth century was an Age of Genocide; it would seem natural, therefore, that we should try to build the means of ensuring that the new century will not go the same way. This is proving to be difficult. Both government organisations and non-governmental agencies have been working to prevent genocide since 1948, but the number of genocidal eruptions has in fact increased during this time.

In looking at whether or not genocide has a future, we must look back at its past – a time when certain groups of people were considered to be the despised of the earth, designated "unworthy" of life.

If we are to develop a satisfactory appreciation of the lessons of this history for today, each individual must stand back, have a look at the facts of the situation, and ask "what does this mean to *me*?" At the moment of our asking, we are automatically confronted with our understanding of where we stand in relation to the rest of society – to what our responsibilities and obligations should be towards that society, and towards the state that claims to represent its interests. We might even find ourselves approaching the ultimate question: "how should I have behaved in the same situation?" – a question that carries much greater weight than the unanswerable, hit-or-miss, and highly irrelevant "how *would* I have behaved?" This is something we will never know until we are confronted by it, and it must be hoped that none of us will ever have to go down that path.

Understanding genocide can help us appreciate that massive and destructive human criminality exists, and that the onus is on all of us to ensure that it is resisted before it gets out of hand. Living in a peaceful environment does not safeguard immunity, and in this sense it is worth remembering that it was only a few short years between the Sarajevo Olympics and the siege of Sarajevo, or between Rwanda-as-a-model-for-Africa and Rwanda-as-a-hell-on-earth.

We must remember that unspeakable human evil can reappear, anywhere – and at any time. Turning away from it, rather than addressing it, betrays democracy, human dignity, and our own destiny. It is incumbent upon us all never to forget the past century, from which we are only just emerging. Moreover, we must show our children why it is in their interests never to forget.

Genocidal evil – a human, not a natural, phenomenon – is not an unstoppable force, and we are not helpless in the face of it. Each citizen must ask him- or herself whether or not it is their responsibility to do something about it. If each of us realises that through our own actions we can make our little corner of the world a better place than it is now, and if each of our efforts can link up over time, we can all appreciate each other more. And that, it should be said, will be a great start.

DISCUSSION QUESTIONS

- In your view, will the next century be likely to see a repeat of the genocidal outbreaks that so characterised the past?
- What measures will need to be adopted in the future in order to ensure that a genocide-free world can be created?
- Does the stopping of genocide depend on the individual, or on states? Is there a place for action from both sectors?

GLOSSARY

Autogenocide: The practice of genocide by a regime against its own people, where the perpetrators and the victims are from the same group.

Colonialism: The establishment, acquisition, and expansion of colonies by those originating elsewhere, in which sovereignty over land is claimed by a foreign state which stamps its social, political, economic, religious, and cultural characteristics onto the acquired territory. Colonialism presumes an unequal relationship between the colonising power and the indigenous population.

Communism: An economic and social system in which all means of production are owned collectively rather than individually. To ensure this, a single authoritarian party controls both politics and the economy.

Convention: A formally written and legally binding international agreement relating to a specific matter of shared concern among states. It creates obligations that the signatories agree to support and carry out.

Crimes against humanity: A legal category within international law that identifies punishable offences of gross violations of human rights, atrocities, and mass murder of non-combatant civilians. Acts that can be considered as crimes against humanity include, but are not confined to, murder, extermination, enslavement, deportation, imprisonment, torture, rape, and persecutions based on political, racial, and religious grounds.

Declaration: A non-binding international statement signifying the individual and collective intention of states to adhere to and honour whatever ideals are outlined therein.

Democracy: A political philosophy guaranteeing civil and political rights for all citizens, providing constitutional limitations on the power of the executive branch of government, and transferring governmental power between parties via constitutionally indicated means.

Dictatorship: A form of absolute rule in which a government is directed by an individual or a small clique, and where the dictator has the power to govern without the consent of those being governed.

Ethnic cleansing: The deliberate policy of rendering an area ethnically homogeneous by using force or intimidation to remove persons of a given group (or groups) from the area. Ethnic cleansing is not to be confused with genocide, as the goal in ethnic cleansing is land acquisition, not group destruction.

Ethnocide: The destruction of the culture of a group without the killing of its population, where members of a group are deprived of their beliefs, customs, traditions, and values as a result of specific actions by a state, an institution, or an outside body.

Expulsion: The forcible removal by government authorities of a lawful resident or group from the territory of a state.

Fascism: A radical authoritarian political movement and system of government based on an extreme form of nationalism, advocating centralisation of authority, rigorous socioeconomic controls, intolerance of opposition, aggressive chauvinism, and racist discourse.

Genocide: As defined by the UN Convention on Genocide 1948, any one of a number of acts committed with intent to destroy, in whole or in part, a national, ethnical, racial, or religious group.

Human rights: Moral principles establishing certain standards of human behaviour, considered to be inalienable, universal, and innate at the time of a person's birth, that are protected legally in domestic and international law. Such rights derive from the core values of the right to life, liberty, and security.

Impunity: Exemption, avoidance, or escape from punishment, penalty, or recrimination for acts that in the normal run of events would have demanded such sanction.

Intentionality: A crucial defining component of the definition of genocide, as articulated in the UN Convention on Genocide, according to which genocide is committed *with intent* to destroy a group.

International law: The body of rules generally regarded and accepted as pertaining to relations between sovereign states. International law can be bilateral (between two parties), multilateral, or involve inter-governmental organisations. International law is usually regulated by organisations endorsed by the global community, for example the International Court of Justice and the International Criminal Court.

Intervention: The forcible or threatened intrusion by a state into the affairs of another in order to end massive human rights violations, involving interference against its sovereign integrity. Unilateral intervention is uncommon, as an unauthorised breach of sovereignty is considered an act of aggressive war.

Massacre: The intentional, indiscriminate, and merciless killing of a large number of people, in a situation of general slaughter, by members of a more powerful group or military force.

Peace: A period of mutual concord between states, or groups of states, during which there is an absence of war or other hostilities. A time of peace is characterised by no violent conflict between states.

Peacekeeping: Activities relating to the preservation of peace, especially the supervision by international forces of a truce between hostile forces. This usually involves the use of military personnel in non-combat roles, for example in monitoring and facilitating the implementation of agreements. These operations are undertaken with the consent of all the major parties involved.

Persecution: The act of systematically mistreating an individual or group, carried out by another group. This implies physical actions (the infliction of suffering, harassment, isolation, imprisonment, fear, or pain) undertaken in a manner designed to injure, aggrieve, or afflict the targeted group or individual.

Pogrom: A term usually associated with mob attacks against Jewish communities, it has also come to be applied more generally when violence takes place against any persecuted group. During much of the twentieth century, the term implied any attack on Jews regardless of the degree of official input, and irrespective of whether or not the attack was spontaneous or planned. The destruction wrought by pogroms varied from situation to situation, and could involve murder, rape, pillage, physical assault, and wanton or random destruction. Pogroms could lead to genocidal massacres.

Racism: The prejudicial belief that biological characteristics such as skin pigmentation, facial features, bone structures, and hair quality are the primary determinant of human abilities, and that the human species is unequally divided along superior and inferior lines based on such attributes. Racism can lead to active forms of discrimination in the areas of politics, society, culture, economics, religion, and the military, and can be expressed through laws, socio-economic exclusion, discrimination, violence, and genocide.

Rape: A crime of sexual assault, in most cases committed by males against females, in which the victim is unlawfully forced, by the threat or use of violence, to have non-consensual sexual intercourse. Rape and sexual slavery are now recognised as crimes against humanity and war crimes, as well as an element of the crime of genocide when the intention is to contribute to the destruction of a targeted group.

Realpolitik: A German term identifying political behaviour based on practical and material factors rather than on theory or idealism, in accordance with the principle that sees the pragmatic and perceived needs of the state taking precedence over those of international law, justice, or morality.

Safe areas: Safe areas are locations established by the UN, clearly designated and cordoned off by neutral military forces and (in theory) respected by all parties to a conflict, where a targeted population, usually civilians, is offered protection from aggression.

Sovereignty: The guiding principle of international relations and a key attribute of statehood since the Peace of Westphalia in 1648. The term is understood to mean that a state, when recognised by other states and defensible, is able to govern itself without interference from others, and that its laws are not subject to oversight from any other legislature. Sovereignty denotes that states possess legal equality, and that no state has the right to intervene in the domestic jurisdiction of another.

Totalitarianism: A system of government in which no political or personal opposition is permitted, demanding total subservience on the part of individuals and institutions to the state. Totalitarian states are comprised of at least some of the following characteristics: a single-party state dominated by a single leader or a small clique; a weapons monopoly; a communications monopoly; a unifying ideology; an economic system that is either centrally directed, or in which the state plays a dominant role; a police presence that has permanently entrenched extraordinary powers of arrest; and the capacity to employ violence in order to uphold the authority of the state.

War: A state of organised, armed conflict between different states, or different groups within a state, that is usually open and declared. War is characterised by aggression and violence, is often prolonged, and is usually waged by military forces fighting against each other. Conflict taking place during war is typified by high mortality, economic and social disruption, and physical devastation in the areas where fighting takes place.

War crimes: Acts committed during armed conflict that violate the international laws, treaties, customs, and practices governing military conflict between belligerent states or parties. War crimes are a legal category within international law, identifying punishable offences for serious violations (so-called "grave breaches") of the accepted international rules of war. War crimes recognise individual criminal responsibility where such violations occur, enshrining the idea that individuals can be held accountable for their own actions during wartime, provided a moral choice was able to be made at the time of the offence.

BIBLIOGRAPHY

Abzug, Robert H., 1985, *Inside the Vicious Heart: Americans and the Liberation of Nazi Concentration Camps*, New York: Oxford University Press.

Acheson-Brown, Daniel G., 2001, "The Tanzanian Invasion of Uganda: A Just War?", *International Third World Studies Journal and Review*, 12: 1–11.

Akçam, Taner, 2006, *A Shameful Act: The Armenian Genocide and the Question of Turkish Responsibility*, New York: Metropolitan Books.

——, 2012, *The Young Turks' Crime Against Humanity: The Armenian Genocide and Ethnic Cleansing in the Ottoman Empire*, Princeton (NJ): Princeton University Press.

Akhavan, Payam, 2013, *Reducing Genocide to Law: Definition, Meaning, and the Ultimate Crime*, Cambridge: Cambridge University Press.

Allen, Beverley, 1996, *Rape Warfare: The Hidden Genocide in Bosnia-Herzegovina and Croatia*, St. Paul (MN): University of Minnesota Press.

Allen, Tim and Koen Vlassenroot (eds), 2010, *The Lord's Resistance Army: Myth and Reality*, London: Zed Books.

Alvarez, Alex, 2014, *Native America and the Question of Genocide*, Lanham (MD): Rowman and Littlefield.

Arad, Yitzhak, 1987, *Belzec, Sobibor, Treblinka: The Operation Reinhard Death Camps*, Bloomington (IN): Indiana University Press.

Armatta, Judith, 2010, *Twilight of Impunity: The War Crimes Trial of Slobodan Milosevic*, Durham (NC): Duke University Press.

Balakian, Peter, 2003, *The Burning Tigris: The Armenian Genocide and America's Response*, New York: HarperCollins.

Ball, Howard, 1999, *Prosecuting War Crimes and Genocide: The Twentieth Century Experience*, Lawrence (KS): University Press of Kansas.

Ballard, John R., 2007, *Triumph of Self-Determination: Operation Stabilise and United Nations Peacemaking in East Timor*, New York: Praeger.

Barnett, Michael, 2002, *Eyewitness to a Genocide: The United Nations and Rwanda*, Ithaca (NY): Cornell University Press.

Bartrop, Paul R., 2000, *Surviving the Camps: Unity in Adversity during the Holocaust*, Lanham (MD): University Press of America.

——, 2002, "The Relationship between War and Genocide in the Twentieth Century: A Consideration," *Journal of Genocide Research*, vol. 4, no. 4 (December 2002), 519–532.

——, 2004, "Punitive Expeditions and Massacres: Gippsland, Colorado, and the Question of Genocide," in A. Dirk Moses (ed.), *Genocide and Settler Society: Frontier Violence and Stolen Indigenous Children in Australian History*, New York: Berghahn Books: 194–214.

——, 2012, *A Biographical Encyclopedia of Contemporary Genocide: Portraits of Evil and Good*, Santa Barbara (CA): ABC-CLIO.

——, 2013, "Political Realism, Sovereignty and Intervention: Is Genocide Prevention Really Possible in a World of Nation States?", in Deborah Mayersen and Annie Pohlman (eds), *Genocide and Mass Atrocities in Asia: Legacies and Prevention*, London: Routledge, 119–135.

——, 2014, *Encountering Genocide: Personal Accounts from Victims, Perpetrators, and Witnesses*, Santa Barbara (CA): ABC-CLIO.

Baruch, Bernard, 1960, *Baruch: The Public Years*, New York: Holt, Reinhart and Winston.

Bar-Zohar, Michael, 1998, *Beyond Hitler's Grasp: The Heroic Rescue of Bulgaria's Jews*, Holbrooke (MA): Adams Media Corporation.

Bass, Gary J., 2000, *Stay the Hand of Vengeance: The Politics of War Crimes Tribunals*, Princeton (NJ): Princeton University Press.

——, 2013, *The Blood Telegram: Nixon, Kissinger, and a Forgotten Genocide*, New York: Alfred A. Knopf.

Bauer, Yehuda, 1982, *A History of the Holocaust*, New York: Franklin Watts.

Beah, Ishmael, 2008, *A Long Way Gone: Memoirs of a Boy Soldier*, New York: Farrar, Straus and Giroux.

Bellamy, Alex J. and Paul D. Williams, 2013, *Providing Peacekeepers: The Politics, Challenges, and Future of United Nations Peacekeeping Contributions*, New York: Oxford University Press.

Bell-Fialkoff, Andrew, 1999, *Ethnic Cleansing*, London: Palgrave Macmillan.

Berenbaum, Michael (ed.), 1992, *A Mosaic of Victims: Non-Jews Persecuted and Murdered by the Nazis*, New York: New York University Press.

Berenbaum, Michael and Abraham J. Peck (eds), 1998, *The Holocaust and History: The Known, the Unknown, the Disputed, and the Re-examined*, Bloomington (IN): Indiana University Press.

Bloxham, Donald, 2005, *The Great Game of Genocide: Imperialism, Nationalism, and the Destruction of the Ottoman Armenians*, Oxford: Oxford University Press.

——, 2009, *The Final Solution: A Genocide*, Oxford: Oxford University Press.

Bloxham, Donald and A. Dirk Moses (eds), 2010, *The Oxford Handbook of Genocide Studies*, Oxford: Oxford University Press.

Bosco, David, 2014, *Rough Justice: The International Criminal Court in a World of Power Politics*, New York: Oxford University Press.

Brackman, Arnold C., 1987, *The Other Nuremberg: The Untold Story of the Tokyo War Crimes Trial*, New York: William Morrow.

Bradsher, Henry S., 1999, *Afghan Communism and Soviet Intervention*, Oxford: Oxford University Press.

Braham, Randolph L., 2000, *The Politics of Genocide: The Holocaust in Hungary* (condensed edition), Detroit (MI): Wayne State University Press.

Braham, Randolph L. with Scott Miller (eds), 1998, *The Nazis' Last Victims: The Holocaust in Hungary*, Detroit (MI): Wayne State University Press.

Breitman, Richard and Allan J. Lichtman, 2013, *FDR and the Jews*, Cambridge (MA): Belknap Press of Harvard University Press.

Bridgman, Jon M., 1981, *The Revolt of the Hereros*, Berkeley (CA): University of California Press.

——, 1990, *The End of the Holocaust: The Liberation of the Camps*, Portland (OR): Areopagitica Press.

Browning, Christopher, 1992, *Ordinary Men: Reserve Police Battalion 101 and the Final Solution in Poland*, New York: HarperCollins.

Bryce, James and Arnold Toynbee, 2005, *The Treatment of Armenians in the Ottoman Empire, 1915–1916: Documents Presented to Viscount Grey of Fallodon by Viscount Bryce* (Ara Sarafian, ed.), 2nd edition, Princeton (NJ) and London: Gomidas Institute.

Byers, Michael, 2005, *War Law: International Law and Armed Conflict*, London: Atlantic Books.

Cameron, Hazel, 2013, *Britain's Hidden Role in the Rwandan Genocide: The Cat's Paw*, Oxford: Routledge.

Campbell, Greg, 2004, *Blood Diamond: Tracing the Deadly Path of the World's Most Precious Stones*, New York: Basic Books.

Carmichael, Cathie, 2009, *Genocide before the Holocaust*, New Haven (CT): Yale University Press.

Chang, Iris, 1997, *The Rape of Nanking: The Forgotten Holocaust of World War II*, New York: Basic Books.

Charny, Israel W. (ed.), 1999, *Encyclopedia of Genocide* (2 vols.), Santa Barbara (CA): ABC-CLIO.

Chary, Frederick B., 1972, *The Bulgarian Jews and the Final Solution, 1940–1944*, Pittsburgh (PA): University of Pittsburgh Press.

Clark, Phil, 2011, *The Gacaca Courts, Post-Genocide Justice and Reconciliation in Rwanda: Justice without Lawyers*, Cambridge: Cambridge University Press.

Clark, Philip and Zachary Kaufman (eds), 2009, *After Genocide: Transitional Justice, Post-Conflict Reconstruction, and Reconciliation in Rwanda and Beyond*, New York: Columbia University Press.

Collins, Robert O., 2008, *A History of Modern Sudan*, Cambridge: Cambridge University Press.

Conot, Robert E., 1993, *Justice at Nuremberg*, New York: HarperCollins.

Conquest, Robert, 1970, *The Nation Killers: The Soviet Deportation of Nationalities*, New York: Macmillan.

——, 1986, *The Harvest of Sorrow: Soviet Collectivization and the Terror-Famine*, New York: Oxford University Press.

Coogan, Tim Pat, 2012, *The Famine Plot: England's Role in Ireland's Greatest Tragedy*, London: Palgrave Macmillan.

Cornwell, John, 1999, *Hitler's Pope: The Secret History of Pius XII*, New York: Viking Press.

Cribb, Robert, 1990, *The Indonesian Killings of 1965: Studies from Java and Bali*, Clayton (Vic.): Monash University Centre of Southeast Asian Studies.

Crowe, David M., 2014, *War Crimes, Genocide, and Justice: A Global History*, New York: Palgrave Macmillan.

Cruvellier, Thierry, 2010, *Court of Remorse: Inside the International Criminal Tribunal for Rwanda*, Madison (WI): University of Wisconsin Press.

Cryer, Robert and Neil Boister, 2008, *The Tokyo International Military Tribunal*, Oxford: Oxford University Press.

Daalder, Ivo H. and Michael E. O'Hanlon, 2001, *Winning Ugly: NATO's War to Save Kosovo*, Washington, DC: Brookings Institution Press.

Dadrian, Vahakn, 1995, *The History of the Armenian Genocide: Ethnic Conflict from the Balkans to Anatolia to the Caucasus*, Providence (RI): Berghahn Books.

Dalin, David G., 2005, *The Myth of Hitler's Pope: Pope Pius XII and His Secret War against Nazi Germany*, Washington, DC, Henry Regnery.

Dallaire, Roméo, with Brent Beardsley, 2003, *Shake Hands with the Devil: The Failure of Humanity in Rwanda*, Toronto: Random House Canada.

Davies, R. W. and Stephen G. Wheatcroft, 2004, *The Years of Hunger: Soviet Agriculture, 1931–1933*, London: Palgrave Macmillan.

Dawidowicz, Lucy S., 1975, *The War Against the Jews: 1933–1945*, London: Weidenfeld and Nicolson.

Des Forges, Alison, 1999, *Leave None to Tell the Story: Genocide in Rwanda*, New York: Human Rights Watch.

Docker, John, 2008, *The Origins of Violence: Religion, History and Genocide*, London: Pluto Press.

Dreschler, Horst, 1980, *"Let us die fighting": The Struggle of the Herero and Nama against German Imperialism, 1884–1915*, London: Zed Press.

Duggan, Christopher, 2013, *Fascist Voices: An Intimate History of Mussolini's Italy*, Oxford: Oxford University Press.

Dunn, James, 2013, "Genocide in East Timor," in Samuel Totten and William S. Parsons (eds), *Centuries of Genocide: Essays and Eyewitness Accounts*, New York: Routledge, 279–315.

Dwork, Deborah and Robert Jan van Pelt, 2002, *Holocaust: A History*, New York: Norton.

Ehle, John, 1997, *Trail of Tears: The Rise and Fall of the Cherokee Nations*, New York: Anchor Books.

Ehrenfreund, Norbert, 2007, *The Nuremberg Legacy: How the Nazi War Crimes Trials Changed the Course of History*, New York: Palgrave Macmillan.

Eichstaedt, Peter, 2009, *First Kill Your Family: Child Soldiers of Uganda and the Lord's Resistance Army*, Chicago (IL): Chicago Review Press.

Erichsen, Casper and David Olusoga, 2010, *The Kaiser's Holocaust: The Forgotten Genocide of the Second Reich and the Colonial Roots of Nazism*, London: Faber and Faber.

Evans, Gareth, 2008, *The Responsibility to Protect: Ending Mass Atrocity Crimes Once and for All*, Washington, DC: Brookings Institution Press.

Ezeh, Mary-Noelle Ethel, 2012, "Genocide by Starvation: The Role of Religious Organizations and the Local Population in Relief Operations in the Nigeria-Biafra War," in Chima J. Korieh (ed.), *The Nigeria-Biafra War: Genocide and the Politics of Memory*, Amherst (NY): Cambria Press, 91–110.

Favez, Jean-Claude, 1999, *The Red Cross and the Holocaust*, Cambridge: Cambridge University Press.

Fein, Helen, 2007, *Human Rights and Wrongs: Slavery, Terror, Genocide*, Boulder (CO): Paradigm Publishers.

Fernandes, Clinton, 2005, *Reluctant Saviour: Australia, Indonesia and the Independence of East Timor*, Melbourne: Scribe.

Fleitz, Frederick H., 2002, *Peacekeeping Fiascoes of the 1990s: Causes, Solutions, and U.S. Interests*, New York: Praeger.

Flint, Julie and Alex de Waal, 2008, *Darfur: A New History of a Long War*, 2nd edition, London: Zed Books.

Forsyth, Frederick, 1977, *The Making of an African Legend: The Biafra Story*, Harmondsworth (UK): Penguin Books.

Fralon, José-Alain, 2001, *A Good Man in Evil Times: The Story of Aristides de Sousa Mendes – The Man who Saved the Lives of Countless Refugees in World War II*, New York: Carroll and Graf.

Friedländer, Saul, 1997, *Nazi Germany and the Jews: The Years of Persecution, 1933–1939*, New York: HarperCollins.

——, 2007, *Nazi Germany and the Jews, 1939–1945: The Years of Extermination*, New York: HarperCollins.

Friedman, Jonathan C. (ed.), 2011, *The Routledge History of the Holocaust*, London: Routledge.

Fritz, Stephen G., 2011, *Ostkrieg: Hitler's War of Extermination in the East*, Lexington (KY): University Press of Kentucky.

Galbraith, Peter W., 2006, *The End of Iraq: How American Incompetence Created a War without End*, New York: Simon and Schuster.

Gardner, P.D., 1990, *Our Founding Murdering Father: Angus McMillan and the Kurnai Tribe of Gippsland, 1839–1865*, Ensay (Victoria): Ngarak Press.

Gberie, Lansana, 2005, *A Dirty War in West Africa: The RUF and the Destruction of Sierra Leone*, Bloomington (IN): Indiana University Press.

Genser, Jared and Bruno Stagno Ugarte (eds), 2014, *The United Nations Security Council in the Age of Human Rights*, Cambridge: Cambridge University Press.

Gilbert, Martin, 1981, *Auschwitz and the Allies*, London: Michael Joseph/Rainbird.
——, 1986, *The Holocaust: A History of the Jews in Europe During the Second World War*, New York: Henry Holt.
——, 2002, *The Righteous: The Unsung Heroes of the Holocaust*, New York: Doubleday.

Goldberger, Leo (ed.), 1987, *The Rescue of the Danish Jews: Moral Courage Under Stress*, New York: New York University Press.

Goldhagen, Daniel Jonah, 2009, *Worse than War: Genocide, Eliminationism, and the Ongoing Assault on Humanity*, New York: Public Affairs Press.

Gooch, John, 2007, *Mussolini and His Generals: The Armed Forces and Fascist Foreign Policy, 1922–1940*, Cambridge: Cambridge University Press.

Gould, Michael, 2012, *The Struggle for Modern Nigeria: The Biafra War 1967–1970*, London: I.B. Tauris.

Graber, G. S., 1996, *Caravans to Oblivion: The Armenian Genocide, 1915*, New York: John Wiley.

Hallie, Philip P., 1994, *Lest Innocent Blood be Shed: The Story of the Village of Le Chambon and How Goodness Happened There*, New York: Harper.

Hayes, Peter and John K. Roth (eds), 2010, *The Oxford Handbook of Holocaust Studies*, Oxford: Oxford University Press.

Hazan, Pierre, 2004, *Justice in the Time of War: The True Story Behind the International Criminal Tribunal for the Former Yugoslavia*, College Station (TX): Texas A & M University Press.

Henig, Ruth, 2010, *The League of Nations*, London: Haus Publishing.

Hett, Benjamin Carter, 2014, *Burning the Reichstag: An Investigation into the Third Reich's Enduring Mystery*, New York: Oxford University Press.

Hilberg, Raul, 2003, *The Destruction of the European Jews* (3 vols.), New Haven (CT): Yale University Press.

Hiltermann, J.R., 2007, *A Poisonous Affair: America, Iraq, and the Gassing of Halabja*, Cambridge: Cambridge University Press.

Hirsch, Herbert, 2002, *Anti-Genocide: Building an American Movement to Prevent Genocide*, Westport (CT): Prager.

Holbrooke, Richard, 1998, *To End a War*, New York: Random House.

Honig, Jan Willem and Norbert Both, 1997, *Srebrenica: Record of a War Crime*, New York: Penguin Books.

Horvitz, Leslie Alan and Christopher Catherwood, 2006, *Encyclopedia of War Crimes and Genocide*, New York and London: Facts on File.

ICISS (International Commission on Intervention and State Sovereignty), 2001, *The Responsibility to Protect: Report of the International Commission on Intervention and State Sovereignty*, Ottawa: International Development Research Centre.

Jackson, Robert, 2007, *Sovereignty: The Evolution of an Idea*, London: Polity.

Jahan, Rounaq, 2013, "The Bangladesh Genocide," in Samuel Totten and William S. Parsons (eds), *Centuries of Genocide: Essays and Eyewitness Accounts*, New York: Routledge, 249–276.

Johnson, Douglas H., 2003, *The Root Causes of Sudan's Civil Wars*, 2nd edition, Bloomington (IN): Indiana University Press.

Jones, Adam, 2010, *Genocide: A Comprehensive Introduction*, 2nd edition, New York: Routledge.

Jones, Nicholas A., 2010, *The Courts of Genocide: Politics and the Rule of Law in Rwanda and Arusha*, Oxford: Routledge.

Judah, Tim, 2002, *Kosovo: War and Revenge*, New Haven (CT): Yale University Press.

——, 2008, *Kosovo: What Everyone Needs to Know*, Oxford: Oxford University Press.

Kapila, Mukesh, 2013, *Against a Tide of Evil: How One Man Became a Whistleblower to the First Mass Murder of the Twenty-First Century*, Edinburgh: Mainstream Publishing.

Kegley, Charles W., Jr. and Gregory A. Raymond, 2001, *Exorcising the Ghost of Westphalia: Building World Order in the New Millennium*, New York: Pearson.

Kelly, Michael J., 2008, *Ghosts of Halabja: Saddam Hussein and the Kurdish Genocide*, Westport (CT): Praeger.

Kerr, Rachel, 2004, *The International Criminal Tribunal for the Former Yugoslavia: An Exercise in Law, Politics, and Diplomacy*, Oxford: Oxford University Press.

Kershaw, Ian, 2008, *Hitler, Germans, and the Final Solution*, New Haven (CT): Yale University Press.

Kiernan, Ben, 2004, *How Pol Pot Came to Power: Colonialism, Nationalism and Communism in Cambodia, 1930–1975*, 2nd edition, New Haven (CT): Yale University Press.

——, 2007, *Blood and Soil: A World History of Genocide and Extermination from Sparta to Darfur*, New Haven (CT): Yale University Press.

——, 2008, *The Pol Pot Regime: Race, Power, and Genocide in Cambodia under the Khmer Rouge, 1975–79*, 3rd edition, New Haven (CT): Yale University Press.

Knock, Thomas J., 1992, *To End all Wars: Woodrow Wilson and the Quest for a New World Order*, New York: Oxford University Press.

Kolb, Robert, 2013, *The International Court of Justice*, Oxford: Hart Publishing.

Krammer, Arnold, 2010, *War Crimes, Genocide, and the Law: A Guide to the Issues*, Santa Barbara (CA): Praeger.

Kroslak, Daniela, 2007, *The French Betrayal of Rwanda*, Bloomington (IN): Indiana University Press.

Kuper, Leo, 1981, *Genocide: Its Political Use in the Twentieth Century*, New Haven (CT): Yale University Press.

Laqueur, Walter (ed.), 2001, *The Holocaust Encyclopedia*, New Haven (CT): Yale University Press.

Leezenburg, Michiel, 2013, "The *Anfal* Operations in Iraqi Kurdistan," in Samuel Totten and William S. Parsons (eds), *Centuries of Genocide: Essays and Eyewitness Accounts*, New York: Routledge, 395–419.

Lemarchand, René (ed.), 2011, *Forgotten Genocides: Oblivion, Denial, and Memory*, Philadelphia (PA): University of Pennsylvania Press.

Lemkin, Raphael, 1944, *Axis Rule in Occupied Europe: Laws of Occupation, Analysis of Government, Proposals for Redress*, Washington, DC: Carnegie Endowment for International Peace.

Levenson, Claude, 2011, "Tibet: A Neo-Colonial Genocide," in René Lemarchand (ed.), *Forgotten Genocides: Oblivion, Denial, and Memory*, Philadelphia (PA): University of Pennsylvania Press, 91–105.

Levin, Nora, 1968, *The Holocaust: The Destruction of European Jewry, 1933–1945*, New York: Thomas Y. Crowell.

Levine, Hillel, 2012, *In Search of Sugihara: The Elusive Japanese Diplomat who Risked his Life to Rescue 10,000 Jews from the Holocaust*, Lexington (MA): Plunkett Lake Press.

Lewy, Guenter, 2000, *The Nazi Persecution of the Gypsies*, Oxford: Oxford University Press.

Lidegaard, Bo, 2013, *Countrymen*, New York: Alfred A. Knopf.

Longerich, Peter, 2010, *Holocaust: The Nazi Persecution and Murder of the Jews*, Oxford: Oxford University Press.

Maga, Tim, 2001, *Judgment at Tokyo: The Japanese War Crimes Trials*, Lexington (KY): University Press of Kentucky.

Malcolm, Noel, 1996, *Bosnia: A Short History*, New York: New York University Press.

Margolin, Jean-Loius, 1999, "China: A Long March into Night," in Stéphane Courtois, Nicolas Werth, Jean-Louis Panné, Andrzej Paczkowski, Karel Bartosek and Jean-Louis Margolin (eds), *The Black Book of Communism: Crimes, Terror, Repression*, Cambridge (MA): Harvard University Press, 463–546.

Markusen, Eric and David Kopf, 1995, *The Holocaust and Strategic Bombing: Genocide and Total War in the Twentieth Century*, Boulder (CO): Westview Press.

Marshall, Ingeborg, 1998, *A History and Ethnography of the Beothuk*, Montreal and Kingston: McGill-Queen's University Press.

Meisler, Stanley, 2011, *United Nations: A History*, 2nd edition, New York: Grove Press.

Melson, Robert, 1992, *Revolution and Genocide: On the Origins of the Armenian Genocide and the Holocaust*, Chicago (IL): University of Chicago Press.

Melvern, Linda, 2000, *A People Betrayed: The Role of the West in Rwanda's Genocide*, London: Zed Books.

——, 2004, *Conspiracy to Murder: The Rwandan Genocide*, London: Verso.

Mennecke, Martin, 2013, "Genocidal Violence in the Former Yugoslavia: Bosnia Herzegovina and Kosovo," in Samuel Totten and William S. Parsons (eds), *Centuries of Genocide: Essays and Eyewitness Accounts*, New York: Routledge, 477–511.

Mikaberidze, Alexander, 2013, *Atrocities, Massacres, and War Crimes: An Encyclopedia*, Santa Barbara (CA): ABC-CLIO.

Milloy, John S., 1999, *A National Crime: The Canadian Government and the Residential School System, 1879–1986*, Winnipeg: University of Manitoba Press.

Milton, Giles, 2008, *Paradise Lost: Smyrna, 1922*, New York: Basic Books.

Minear, Richard R., 1971, *Victors' Justice: The Tokyo War Crimes Trial*, Princeton (NJ): Princeton University Press.

Mojzes, Paul, 2011, *Balkan Genocides: Holocaust and Ethnic Cleansing in the Twentieth Century*, Lanham (MD): Rowman and Littlefield.

Morgenthau, Henry, 2003, *Ambassador Morgenthau's Story*, ed. Peter Balakian, Detroit (MI): Wayne State University Press.

Morsink, Johannes, 2000, *The Universal Declaration of Human Rights: Origins, Drafting, and Intent*, Philadelphia (PA): University of Pennsylvania Press.

Mortimer, Rex, 2007, *Indonesian Communism under Sukarno: Ideology and Politics, 1959–1965*, Farminton (MO): Solstice Publishing.

Moses, A. Dirk (ed.), 2004, *Genocide and Settler Society: Frontier Violence and Stolen Indigenous Children in Australian History*, New York: Berghahn.

Naimark, Norman M., 2001, *Fires of Hatred: Ethnic Cleansing in Twentieth Century Europe*, Cambridge (MA): Harvard University Press.

——, 2010, *Stalin's Genocides*, Princeton (NJ): Princeton University Press.

Neufeld, Michael J. and Michael Berenbaum (eds), 2000, *The Bombing of Auschwitz: Should the Allies have Attempted it?* New York: St. Martin's Press.

Nevins, Joseph, 2005, *A Not-So-Distant Horror: Mass Violence In East Timor*, Ithaca (NY): Cornell University Press.

Nuhanović, Hasan, 2007, *Under the UN Flag: The International Community and the Srebrenica Genocide*, Sarajevo: DES Sarajevo.

Nye, Joseph S., Jr., 2004, *Soft Power: The Means to Success in World Politics*, New York: PublicAffairs Press.

Off, Carol, 2000, *The Lion, the Fox and the Eagle: A Story of Generals and Justice in Yugoslavia and Rwanda*, Toronto: Random House.

Ó Gráda, Cormac, 2000, *Black '47 and Beyond: The Great Irish Famine in History, Economy, and Memory*, Princeton (NJ): Princeton University Press.

Paldiel, Mordecai, 1993, *The Path of the Righteous: Gentile Rescuers of Jews during the Holocaust*, New York: KTAV.

——, 2000, *Saving the Jews: Amazing Stories of Men and Women who Defied the "Final Solution"*, Rockville (MD): Schreiber Publishing.

Peterson, Jacqueline and Jennifer S.H. Brown (eds), 2001, *The New Peoples: Being and Becoming Métis in North America*, St. Paul (MN): Minnesota Historical Society Press.

Petterson, Donald, 2003, *Inside Sudan: Political Islam, Conflict, and Catastrophe*, rev. ed., New York: Basic Books.

Pigott, Peter, 2009, *Canada in Sudan: War without Borders*, Toronto: Dundurn Press.

Pohl, J. Otto, 1999, *Ethnic Cleansing in the USSR, 1937–1949*, New York: Praeger.

Power, Samantha, 2002, *"A Problem from Hell": America and the Age of Genocide*, New York: Basic Books.

Priemel, Kim C. and Alexa Stiller (eds), 2012, *Reassessing the Nuremberg Military Tribunals: Transitional Justice, Trial Narratives, and Historiography*, New York: Berghahn Books.

Prunier, Gérard, 1997, *The Rwanda Crisis: History of a Genocide*, New York: Columbia University Press.

——, 2008a, *Darfur: A 21st Century Genocide*, 3rd edition, Ithaca (NY): Cornell University Press.

——, 2008b, *Africa's World War: Congo, the Rwandan Genocide and the Making of a Continental Catastrophe*, New York: Oxford University Press.

Reeves, Eric, 2007, *A Long Day's Dying: Critical Moments in the Darfur Genocide*, Toronto: The Key Publishing House.

Reitlinger, Gerald, 1956, *The SS, Alibi of a Nation*, London: William Heinemann.

Reynolds, Henry, 2001, *An Indelible Stain? The Question of Genocide in Australia's History*, Melbourne: Viking Australia.

——, 2013, *A Forgotten War*, Sydney: NewSouth.

Rittner, Carol and John K. Roth (eds), 2012, *Rape: Weapon of War and Genocide*, St. Paul (MN): Paragon House.

Robinson, Geoffrey, 2010, *"If you leave us here, we will die": How Genocide was Stopped in East Timor*, Princeton (NJ): Princeton University Press.

Rohde, David, 1997, *Endgame: The Betrayal and Fall of Srebrenica, Europe's Worst Massacre since World War II*, New York: Farrar, Straus and Giroux.

Rubenstein, Richard L., 1983, *The Age of Triage: Fear and Hope in an Overcrowded World*, Boston (MA): Beacon Press.

Rummel, R. J., 1990, *Lethal Politics: Soviet Genocide and Mass Murder Since 1917*, New Brunswick (NJ): Transaction Publishers.

——, 1991, *China's Bloody Century: Genocide and Mass Murder Since 1900*, New Brunswick (NJ): Transaction Publishers.

——, 1997, *Death by Government*, New Brunswick (NJ): Transaction Publishers.

——, 2002, *Power Kills: Democracy as a Method of Nonviolence*, New Brunswick (NJ): Transaction Publishers.

Ryan, Lyndall, 1981, *The Aboriginal Tasmanians*, St. Lucia (Queensland): University of Queensland Press.

Sarkin, Jeremy, 2010, *Germany's Genocide of the Herero: Kaiser Wilhelm II, His General, His Settlers, His Soldiers*, Cape Town: UCT Press.

Sassoon, Joseph, 2011, *Saddam Hussein's Ba'th Party: Inside an Authoritarian Regime*, New York: Cambridge University Press.

Schabas, William A., 2006, *The UN International Criminal Tribunals: The Former Yugoslavia, Rwanda and Sierra Leone*, Cambridge: Cambridge University Press.

——, 2009, *Genocide in International Law: The Crime of Crimes*, 2nd edition, Cambridge: Cambridge University Press.

——, 2011, *An Introduction to the International Criminal Court*, 4th edition, Cambridge: Cambridge University Press.

Schwab, Gerald, 1990, *The Day the Holocaust Began: The Odyssey of Herschel Grynszpan*, New York: Praeger.

Segev, Tom 2009, "When Tel Aviv was a Wilderness," www.haaretz.com, October 5, 2009.

Shaw, Martin, 2007, *What is Genocide?*, London: Polity Press.

Shawcross, William, 1979, *Sideshow: Kissinger, Nixon and the Destruction of Cambodia*, New York: Simon and Schuster.

Shelton, Dinah (ed.), 2004, *Encyclopedia of Genocide and Crimes against Humanity* (3 vols.), New York: Macmillan.

Short, Philip, 2006, *Pol Pot: Anatomy of a Nightmare*, New York: Holt.

Slim, Hugo, 2007, *Killing Civilians: Method, Madness and Morality in War*, London: Hurst.

Smith, Adam M., 2009, *After Genocide: Bringing the Devil to Justice*, Amherst (NY): Prometheus Books.

Smith, Bradley F., 1981, *The Road to Nuremberg*, New York: Basic Books.

Solis, Gary D., 2010, *The Law of Armed Conflict: International Humanitarian Law in War*, New York: Cambridge University Press.

Stannard, David E., 1993, *American Holocaust: Columbus and the Conquest of the New World*, New York: Oxford University Press.

Stearns, Jason K., 2011, *Dancing in the Glory of Monsters: The Collapse of the Congo and the Great War of Africa*, New York: PublicAffairs Press.

Steidle, Brian with Gretchen Steidle Wallace, 2007, *The Devil Came on Horseback: Bearing Witness to the Genocide in Darfur*, New York: PublicAffairs.

Stiglmayer, Alexandra (ed.), 1994, *Mass Rape: The War against Women in Bosnia-Herzegovina*, Lincoln (NE): University of Nebraska Press.

Stremlau, John J., 1977, *The International Politics of the Nigerian Civil War, 1967–1970*, Princeton (NJ): Princeton University Press.

Suny, Ronald Grigor, Fatma Muge Göçek, and Norman M. Naimark (eds), 2011, *A Question of Genocide: Armenians and Turks at the End of the Ottoman Empire*, Oxford: Oxford University Press.

Tams, Christian J. and James Sloan (eds), 2013, *The Development of International Law by the International Court of Justice*, Oxford: Oxford University Press.

Taylor, Telford, 1992, *The Anatomy of the Nuremberg Trials: A Personal Memoir*, New York: Alfred A. Knopf.

Tec, Nechama, 2013, *Resistance: Jews and Christians who Defied the Nazi Terror*, New York: Oxford University Press.

Temple-Raston, Dina, 2008, *Justice on the Grass: Three Rwandan Journalists, Their Trial for War Crimes and a Nation's Quest for Redemption*, New York: Free Press.

Thompson, Allan (ed.), 2007, *The Media and the Rwanda Genocide*, London: Pluto Press.

Totani, Yuma, 2008, *The Tokyo War Crimes Trial: The Pursuit of Justice in the Wake of World War II*, Cambridge (MA): Harvard University Press.

Totten, Samuel and Eric Markusen (eds), 2006, *Genocide in Darfur: Investigating the Atrocities in the Sudan*, New York: Routledge.

Totten, Samuel and Paul R. Bartrop (with contributions by Steven Leonard Jacobs), 2008, *Dictionary of Genocide* (2 vols.), Westport (CT): Greenwood Press.

Totten, Samuel and Paul R. Bartrop, 2009, *The Genocide Studies Reader*, New York: Routledge.

Travis, Hannibal, 2010, *Genocide in the Middle East: The Ottoman Empire, Iraq, and Sudan*, Durham (NC): Carolina Academic Press.

Vági, Zoltán, László Csősz, and Gábor Kádár, 2013, *The Holocaust in Hungary: Evolution of a Genocide*, Lanham (MD): AltaMira Press.

Waller, James, 2002, *Becoming Evil: How Ordinary People Commit Genocide and Mass Killing*, Oxford: Oxford University Press.

Wallis, Andrew, 2007, *Silent Accomplice: The Untold Story of France's Role in the Rwandan Genocide*, London: I. B. Tauris.

Waters, Timothy William, 2014, *The Milosevic Trial: An Autopsy*, New York: Oxford University Press.

Weale, Adrian, 2012, *Army of Evil: A History of the SS*, New York: NAL Caliber.

Weart, Spencer R., 2000, *Never at War: Why Democracies will not Fight One Another*, New Haven (CT): Yale University Press.

Weymouth, Tony and Stanley Henig (eds), 2001, *The Kosovo Crisis: The Last American War in Europe?*, London: Reuters.

Woodham-Smith, Cecil, 1962, *The Great Hunger: Ireland 1845–1849*, New York: Harper and Row.

Yahil, Leni, 1990, *The Holocaust: The Fate of European Jewry, 1932–1945*, New York: Oxford University Press.

Zuccotti, Susan, 2002, *Under His Very Windows: The Vatican and the Holocaust in Italy*, New Haven (CT): Yale University Press.

INDEX

Arabic names are indexed under the second element; e.g al-Bashir is listed
under B